Greetings to a comrade
in the war for peace!

—

John Haynes Holmes
The Community Church
New York City

═

IF THIS BE TREASON

John Francis Goldsmith
Easton, Pennsylvania

THE MACMILLAN COMPANY
NEW YORK · BOSTON · CHICAGO · DALLAS
ATLANTA · SAN FRANCISCO

MACMILLAN & CO., Limited
LONDON · BOMBAY · CALCUTTA
MELBOURNE

THE MACMILLAN COMPANY
OF CANADA, Limited
TORONTO

IF THIS BE TREASON

A Play in Three Acts and Seven Scenes

BY JOHN HAYNES HOLMES
AND
REGINALD LAWRENCE

NEW YORK
THE MACMILLAN COMPANY
1935

Set up and printed. Published, October, 1935.

This play was produced by the Theatre Guild, under the direction of Harry Wagstaff Gribble, at the Music Box Theatre, New York, on September 23, 1935. It was the first play of the Guild season of 1935-1936.

SET UP BY BROWN BROTHERS LINOTYPERS
PRINTED IN THE UNITED STATES OF AMERICA
BY THE FERRIS PRINTING COMPANY

INTRODUCTION

I

THE subject of this play is the will of the peoples of the world to peace. Its hero is not John Gordon, President of the United States, nor Koyé, popular leader of the Japanese masses, but the common men and women whose hidden desires they express and whose latent energies they release. Its thesis is the simple proposition that if the people of any two countries involved in a war crisis were only given by their governments the same opportunity to serve the interests of peace that they are invariably given to serve the interests of war, peace and not war would come.

The plot and purpose of the play are clearly stated in the scene between President Gordon and Secretary of State Dickinson, in Act II, where the following dialogue occurs:

GORDON. I'm counting on the people.
DICKINSON. They're mad.
GORDON. Because they've been bitten by mad dogs.
Well, I've got a cure for that.

DICKINSON. What cure?

GORDON. I'll give them just as good a chance to get excited about peace as Brainard has given them to get excited about war.

DICKINSON. People care precious little about peace in a situation like this.

GORDON. Did you ever stop to think, Dickinson, why people always choose war in a crisis? Because they're never given an opportunity to choose anything else. The moment trouble begins, press, politicians, pulpits start baying for war. . . . But what if peace had a decent chance? What if people were asked *not* to fight as urgently as they are now asked to fight?

II

The setting of the play, a pacifist President confronted by a war crisis, is neither important nor original. Ever since I can remember, this theme has been a commonplace of pacifist discussion. It received literary expression as early as 1913 in Frank Copley's interesting book, *The Impeachment of President Israel.*[1] It was given a permanent historical basis by the tragic experience of President Wilson in 1914-1917, in failing to keep America out of the Great War in accordance with

[1] Published by Macmillan. This book, widely read but now out of print, remains a classic in the pacifist literature of our time.

his own basic principles and ideals of peace. In all argument, however, of this problem, in which I have engaged and have heard others engage, there has been missing any constructive solution of the dilemma. It was always easy to tell what a pacifist President in a war crisis should *not* do—namely, not take his country into war. But it was never easy to tell what he *should* do. A negative policy, mere inaction, was not enough to win and hold popular support and thus swing the people to the side of peace. Nor was it enough merely to say that the President should make terms with the enemy. How should he make such terms? Just what, for example, should President Wilson have done to keep us out of war in 1917? Through all the early scenes in this play, when war is crashing down upon the nation, President Gordon is trying and failing to find "a way to peace." Where is this "way"?

For years I could discover no answer to this question in terms of practical statesmanship. Then, in 1931, I had an experience which seemed to reveal the solution of the problem. It was in September of that year that I saw Gandhi, of India, come to England to meet the Prime Minister and the King. I was at Folkstone when the Mahatma arrived, and greeted him as he set foot on English soil. I was with him in London for a week—at the Friends Meeting House where he addressed a great audience of Englishmen, at Kingsley Hall where he lived among the English slum-dwellers, at St. James Palace where he conferred with British cabinet ministers. I came to think of him as the third in the succession of Julius Cæsar and William of Normandy as conquerors of Britain. For more than a decade, Gandhi had been carrying on his non-violent resistance conflict with the British Crown in his native country, India. In this conflict he had suffered arrest, imprisonment, torture, but had proved himself the most formidable foe that Britain had encountered in all her history as an empire. Now, after meeting face to face with the Viceroy in Delhi, this amazing man had come *to his enemy's country,* to meet those with whom he had been contending, and to seek peace in the name of their people and his own.

In this unprecedented episode I seemed to discover a new and triumphant method of preventing a war precipitated by conflicting interests, strange accidents, and irresponsible militaristic policies of government. It was the seed suggestion, as it later became the full-flowered thesis, of my play. It was on my voyage home across the Atlantic, after my unforgettable week with Mahatma, that I conceived the first outline of "If This Be Treason."

III

If the visit of Gandhi to London, in 1931, was the basis of this play as unfolded in the climactic scenes of Act III, in which President Gordon is found in Tokio in conference with the Japanese Premier, Yato, other historical characters and episodes served as the basis of other elements in the story. I would make these plain, that this drama may be correctly seen, not as a mere idealistic fantasy but rather as a serious essay in realism.

Thus, to those familiar with contemporary Japan it must be obvious that the Japanese revolutionary, Koyé, is nothing more nor less than a dramatic projection of the famous Kagawa. The career of this man, one of the noblest of our time, can be matched in spiritual significance and public importance only by that of Gandhi himself. A Christian convert, utterly dedicated in thought and life to the Tolstoian conception of his faith, Kagawa has for years been preaching his pacifist gospel to the multitudinous poor of the cities and villages in his native land. As an essential part of this activity, he has organized the Japanese workers in trade unions, led great movements of political and social reform, and among the young people especially has toiled unremittingly for peace. It is not only easy but inevitable to see the logic of such a life leading in the end to what is depicted in Act III of the play.

The scene of President Gordon and Admiral James, in Act II, is a deliberate adaptation of the famous interview of Field-Marshal von Moltke with Wilhelm II on the eve of the Great War, when a misapprehension that France might remain neutral under an English guarantee induced the Kaiser to scrap the Schlieffen plan for war and order the whole German army thrown against the Russians. "That is impossible, Your Majesty," said Moltke. "An army of a million men cannot be improvised. . . . It is utterly impossible to advance except according to plan." Kaiser Wilhelm yielded to the inflexibility of the war machine, as President Gordon did not, announcing that "for technical reasons the mobilization on two fronts, ordered by me this afternoon, . . . cannot now be countermanded." Moltke, describing the interview, declared he was "like a broken man, and shed tears of despair." [2]

The following scene in Act III, the meeting of the Congressional Committee with President Gordon, was suggested by the meeting of the Senate Foreign Relations Committee with President Woodrow Wilson on his first return from the peace conferences in Paris. This committee on the stage

[2] See Emil Ludwig, *Kaiser Wilhelm II,* the latest and most accessible version of an historic episode.

of history was as hostile to President Wilson's peace plans as the imagined committee on the stage of this play is hostile to President Gordon's peace plans. The two scenes are in essentials identical.

The final and decisive episode of the play, the uprising of the Japanese populace, has been criticized as incredible, yet, like these other episodes, it is based on fact—the historic fact of revolution, or more particularly in this case, of the Russian Revolution. This fact is the commonplace, incredible only because it never happens until it *happens,* that an unarmed crowd, impelled by a long-sustained campaign of agitation, can overcome an army when the army is itself unwilling to defend the government. Revolutions break at that terrific moment when soldiers refuse to fire upon the people.

Thus, Hilaire Belloc, in his *The French Revolution,* refers to "the absurd conception that any body of men in uniform, however small, can always have the better of civilian resistance. . . . The truth is that in dealing with large bodies of men (civilians), the issue (as between army and people) will always be doubtful, and the uncertain factor is one that varies within the very widest limits."

Arthur Bullard, describing the outbreak of the Russian Revolution,[3] records that "large numbers

[3] In his *The Russian Pendulum.*

of troops were brought to Petrograd, the police were heavily armed. . . . But when the people came out on the streets, the troops refused to fire on them."

Leon Trotsky has described the process thus at work.[4] "There is no doubt," he writes, "that the fate of every revolution at a certain point is decided by a break in the disposition of the army. Against a numerous, disciplined, well-armed, and ably led military force, unarmed or almost unarmed masses of the people cannot gain a victory. But no deep national victory can fail to affect the army to some extent. The psychological moment when the soldiers go over to the revolution . . . has its point of climax. . . . The more the soldiers in their mass are convinced that the rebels are really rebelling, that the people may win if they join them, the more willing they are to turn aside their bayonets. . . . The critical hour has its critical minute, . . . when the officer gives the command 'Fire,' and the rifles waver. . . . This decides not only the fate of the street skirmish, but perhaps the whole day, or the whole insurrection."

It is precisely such an incident which is depicted at the close of Act III as the "critical minute" of the play.

[4] In his *The History of the Russian Revolution.*

IV

It is in this sense that practically all the scenes in "If This Be Treason" are based on actual events of history. The material used throughout by my collaborator and myself is not fantastic but realistic. What is probable or improbable in our world? If any dramatist had written a play about the story of Nicolai Lenin from the utter obscurity in 1914 of a Russian refugee to the supreme triumph in 1917 of a Russian ruler, would he not have been accused of an extravagance infinitely greater than anything suggested by the tale of President Gordon?

War some day will be abolished by the will of man. This assertion does not in any way invalidate the truth that war is fundamentally caused by impersonal political, economic and social forces—in our day predominantly economic. But it is the destiny of man to master and control such forces, even as it is his destiny to harness rivers, chain the lightning, and ride the storm. It is human will, operating upon social forces, that has abolished slavery, infanticide, duelling, and a score of other social enormities. Why should it not eventually do the same with war?

The day will come! And when it comes, the decisive moment will be signalized by just such a dramatic gesture by a great and brave statesman as is projected in this play.

V

My first acknowledgments must go to my esteemed friend and collaborator, Reginald Lawrence, co-author of "Men Must Fight" and other plays, whose self-effacing, devoted and effective workmanship turned my manuscript into a script for the theatre. Other acknowledgments, touched with gratitude and high personal regard, are due to Lawrence Langner, president of the Theatre Guild, who believed in this play from the start; to Harry Wagstaff Gribble, whose skilful and tireless labors as director turned a script into a living drama; and to McKaye Morris and the large company of actors who gave their artistic abilities and experience to this play with an enthusiasm which could not have been greater had the play been their own.

Lastly, a reverent salutation to the Theatre Guild—its directors, officers, and representatives!

JOHN HAYNES HOLMES.

SPEAKING CHARACTERS

JOHN GORDON, *President of the United States.*
DOROTHY GORDON, *wife of the President.*
ROBERT GORDON, *his son.*
DUNCAN, *Secretary to the President.*
TURNER, *his Press Secretary.*
MISS FOLWELL, *his Personal Secretary.*
DICKINSON, *Secretary of State.*
FULTON, *Secretary of War.*
ALDRICH, *Secretary of the Navy.*
ADMIRAL JAMES.
BRIGHT, *Senator from Massachusetts.*
HILL, *Senator from California.*
WILMOT, *Representative from Illinois.*
FITZGERALD, *Representative from Wyoming.*
SMITH, *Representative from Georgia.*
BRAINARD, *ex-President of the United States.*
LORD CARRINGTON, *British Ambassador to Japan.*
PRINCE YATO, *Premier of Japan.*
GENERAL NOGATU, *Japan's Minister of War.*
BARON ISHIWARA, *Conference Delegate.*
DR. FUJIMOTO, *Conference Delegate.*
TODU, *Premier Yato's Secretary-Aide.*
KOYÉ, *Leader of the People.*
MRS. BANE, *a Washington Dowager.*
MANSFIELD, *a Young Diplomat.*
M. GIRADAUT, *French Ambassador in Washington.*
BRITISH AMBASSADOR *in Washington.*

SILENT CHARACTERS

ITALIAN AMBASSADOR *in Washington*
MRS. WILMOT
MISS WILMOT
MRS. DICKINSON
MRS. HILL
MRS. SMITH
BRITISH AMBASSADOR'S WIFE
FRENCH AMBASSADOR'S WIFE
FIRST GENERAL
FIRST GENERAL'S WIFE
SECOND GENERAL
SECOND GENERAL'S WIFE
FIRST NAVAL OFFICER
FIRST NAVAL OFFICER'S WIFE
SECOND NAVAL OFFICER
OLD LADY
MESSENGER *from U. S. War Department*
JAPANESE SECRETARY (*girl*)
JAPANESE SECRETARY (*man*)
GUESTS, *men and women, young and old, at the Inaugural Reception. Also servants and lackeys.*
SECRETARIES and SOLDIERS *at the Japanese conference room in Tokio. Also crowd, with leaders.*

ACT ONE

SCENE I

[*The White House. Inauguration Day. Ten o'clock, evening.* DUNCAN'S *rooms.* DUNCAN, *the President's Secretary, a quiet, youngish man, is dressing for the Inaugural Reception.* TURNER, *the Press Secretary, is dressing with him; enters hurriedly from room at right.*]

DUNCAN. We're late as the devil, Turner. The reception'll be over before we get down.

TURNER. Can't help it! I've had that news gang downstairs hanging on my neck since before breakfast. When's the President going to say something?

DUNCAN. He said something this morning.

TURNER. That was this morning. Nobody listens to an inaugural address.

DUNCAN. Did you *hear* President Gordon's address? Or were you in your customary crap game?

TURNER. I heard it. A peace sermon, at a time like this! We'll be at war with Japan in twenty-four hours.

DUNCAN. That remains to be seen. Brainard did

everything he could to get us into war—but there's another man in office tonight.

TURNER. Brainard's still in Washington. That jingo's fired, but he doesn't know it.—Tie this tie, will you?

DUNCAN. Tie it yourself, I'm late.

TURNER. As the President's Secretary, you're as much help as a Siamese twin.

DUNCAN. As the Press Secretary, you're no help at all.—War scare headlines, on the day of Gordon's inauguration! [*Takes up sheet of clippings, shakes them at* TURNER.] Look at them!

TURNER. You flatter me. What have I got to do with headlines, when every paper in the country is featuring Japan's defy to our ultimatum.

DUNCAN. Brainard's ultimatum.

TURNER. *America's* ultimatum. Japan fired on our Embassy at Tokio, and the government called her to account. And Japan "regrets . . .!" My God! She'll regret it all right, when we show her what we've got in the mitt.

DUNCAN. You talk like a Brainard man, Turner.

TURNER. Not me! But I believe in using my fists when I get hit. And Japan certainly took a sock at us with that reply.

DUNCAN. The Japs were right, as it happens. The attack on the Embassy was provoked by our own policies.

TURNER. Provoked or not, it's war—war in any copy book.

DUNCAN. Not in President Gordon's.

TURNER. Listen, Duncan. I'm not blaming you, but you've been working so long for that pacifist that you think he's the Lord God Almighty. Gordon might as well be a gnat in a gale, as a peace President in Washington tonight.

DUNCAN. It's a gale, all right, and it's up to the press department to control it.

TURNER. Look here, Duncan! I'll swap jobs with you this minute. You go down there and try to slip the boys the little valentines I've been offering them all day: "Trust President Gordon to see us through." "President elected on peace platform, we mustn't let him down." "The people must be calm!"—Try and get them to print that stuff, with the army mobilizing and the navy at sea.

DUNCAN. Brainard's orders.

TURNER. Oh, for God's sake, Duncan! It just happened that Japan's reply came through forty-eight hours ago. If it had come through today, Gordon would have had to give those same orders.

DUNCAN. Would he?

TURNER. Well, what else could he have done?

DUNCAN. Just what he's doing now. Taking time

to breathe, and not letting his tongue run away with his brain!

TURNER. But he's got to make a statement. He's not Cal Coolidge, you know. He can't *choose* not to speak.

DUNCAN. He chose not to mention war or Japan in his inaugural address this morning, and that spoke volumes to those who understand.

TURNER. There's not a person in America who can understand pacifism tonight.

DUNCAN. There are plenty—here, and in Japan too.

TURNER. Pacifists in Japan? Say, Duncan, you're going screwy.

DUNCAN. Oh, am I? Hey, fasten these suspenders.

TURNER. I'm damned if I will.

DUNCAN. What about Koyé?

TURNER. Koyé? That fanatic!

DUNCAN. Call him what you like! Premier Yato's got his own yellow peril right in Tokio.

TURNER. Koyé's as crazy as Gandhi of India.

DUNCAN. So you think Gandhi's crazy? Well, consult the British Empire about that!—Koyé has followers everywhere—workers, students . . .

TURNER. Students!—The pen mightier than the sword, eh?

DUNCAN. They made good fighters before, you

may remember, when we had our little trouble with Germany.—By the way, Turner, what did you do in the last war?

TURNER. Raised potatoes and cut out sugar. What did you do?

DUNCAN. Went to school, studied civil liberties, and made coal out of newspaper pulp—for democracy. [*Telephone rings. He answers it.*] Hello? Duncan, the President's Secretary. . . . Yes, Senator Bright. . . . I can't disturb the President now, sir. He'll be down as soon as he's dressed. . . . Rather tired, I suppose, naturally. He's never been inaugurated before. . . . An appointment? . . . To see him early tomorrow? He'll be pretty busy, of course. His first day in office, you know. But he'll want to see you if he can. . . . A committee? What committee, Senator? . . . Oh, of Congress. [TURNER *shows interest.*] I see. . . . Well, I'll tell the President, Senator. And of course he'll arrange to see the committee somehow. . . . Yes, Senator. [TURNER *is making signs.*] Oh, one minute, please. Mr. Turner, the Press Secretary, is here. He'd like to speak to you. [*He hands the 'phone to* TURNER.]

TURNER. Good evening, Senator Bright. Have you got some statement about that committee? . . . Oh. . . . A *personal* statement! All right,

Senator. . . . "The people of Massachusetts want war." Yes, sir. Have always wanted war. . . . Oh, excuse me, Senator. About that committee. . . . Oh! Yes, sir. "The Revolution. . . . Bunker Hill. . . ."

DUNCAN. Ask him where Massachusetts is.

TURNER. Shut up! . . . Oh, I beg pardon, Senator. . . . Yes, sir. "Every man—every dollar—every gun. Our patience exhausted—our nation insulted." . . . I know exactly how you feel, Senator—"a peace-loving people." *Yes*, sir, I have that. But about this committee to wait on the President? . . . Oh, you have. . . . Oh, you are. . . . Oh, you did. . . . Oh, him too! I see. Nice little gang you've got. Yes, I've got it. I'll try and catch the bulldog edition with that. . . . Thank you, Senator. See you later. Good-bye. [*He hangs up.*]

DUNCAN. You're not going to use any stuff about that fool committee tonight.

TURNER. It's news, Duncan. A committee from Congress demanding war!

DUNCAN. What President Gordon tells the committee will be the news. You keep this out of the papers.

TURNER. Everyone at the reception will hear of it. Fitzgerald, of Wyoming, is on the committee. Do you suppose he can keep that gas-bag of his closed?—Senator Hill of California, won't he talk? And Wilmot, that munitions grafter, he'll be selling machine guns to the orchestra!

DUNCAN. Those damn fire-eaters! It they'd only give Gordon a chance. . . .

TURNER. There isn't a chance to give.

DUNCAN. There will be, when he gets through to the *people*.

TURNER. Listen, Duncan, I'm a press man, don't talk to me about the people. They're as sentimental as hell. When it's peace, they talk about brotherly love, and read books about Russia. When it's war, they yell about dying for the flag, and read Brisbane.

[*Knock on door.*]

DUNCAN. Come in. [*Enter* ROBERT GORDON, *a sturdy boy of thirteen, son of the President. He is in his first dinner coat and trousers, and is whistling happily.*] No whistling, Bob. This is the White House.

ROBERT. [*Stops.*] Yes, Mr. Duncan.

DUNCAN. How are you, Robert? Shake hands with your father's Press Secretary, the unfortunate Mr. Turner.

ROBERT. How do you do, sir.—Say, Mr. Duncan, do they have many dances like this in the White House?

DUNCAN. Sure thing! Come back in four years and we'll have another.

ROBERT. Gee, you mean dad'll get a second term?

TURNER. If he gets over the first one.

DUNCAN. Where is your father?

ROBERT. With mother.—He sent me in to tell you he'd like to see you.—Say, those are swell trousers.

DUNCAN. Not bad.—Let's see yourself. [ROBERT *turns.*] What do you say, Turner. Think they'll suit the ladies?

TURNER. Right down to the ground!—Come ahead, Robert. Let's take a squint at the ladies. Maybe their husbands will stop yelling for war, now that they've changed into boiled shirts.

DUNCAN. I thought you news-hawks wanted a war.

TURNER. Not tonight. That would spoil the picture.—Leave it to Turner to get the new administration off the spot.

ROBERT. The spot?—What's he mean, *"spot"?*

DUNCAN [*gently, almost paternally*]. A spot, Bob, is trouble, a lot of trouble.—Things are happening.

ROBERT. You mean the trouble with Japan. Dad told me about the mob attacking our Embassy. And about the man that shot at the Ambassador, too.

DUNCAN [*soberly*]. Did he tell you about Mr. Brainard's ultimatum?

ROBERT. Yes, sir, he did.

TURNER. What did he say?

ROBERT [*turning to* TURNER]. He said an ultimatum was where a fellow put a stick on his shoulder and dared you to knock it off.

TURNER. And that's what Japan did, my boy. Knocked it off.

DUNCAN. He means, Robert, that Japan sent an unfortunate reply.—And yesterday the fleet put to sea, and the army units started mobilizing at San Francisco.

ROBERT [*somewhat awed*]. Does that mean war, Mr. Duncan?

DUNCAN. Not necessarily. But it's trouble, Robert. That's what Mr. Turner meant when he said your father is on a spot. But don't you be afraid. You stand by your father, as I do. He'll get out of it, if any man can.—Come along, we'll go down and see him. [*Opens the door.*]

TURNER. Hey, shut that door a minute. [*Takes out a flask, and swallows a quick drink.*]

ROBERT [*wondering*]. What's that?

DUNCAN. That's a flask.—Mr. Turner forgets that Prohibition was repealed, and that this is a free country.

TURNER. So I've read. But I've got to have more

of a kick than I'll get out of that pink punch downstairs. [*Takes another swallow.*] To another Noble Experiment, God bless it!

END OF SCENE ONE

SCENE II

[*The White House.* PRESIDENT GORDON'S *private drawing-room. Evening of Inauguration Day, just after close of Scene I.* GORDON, DUNCAN, ROBERT; *also* MISS FOLWELL, *an attractive and sensible young woman.* GORDON *is a tall, handsome, distinguished-looking man of between forty and fifty years of age, whose carriage and manner of humorous sympathy conceal his worry and fatigue. He stands at the fireplace, at the front of the stage, back to the audience.* DUNCAN *is facing the* PRESIDENT, *holding a card of pasted clippings.* ROBERT *and* MISS FOLWELL *are about to leave.*]

GORDON. [*Hands paper to* DUNCAN.] That's all right, Duncan.

FOLWELL. Oh, Mr. President, I have word from

the Navy Department. The Secretary of the Navy will probably not be able to attend the reception tonight.

GORDON. I'm sorry. I wanted Aldrich to be here. I wanted the whole Cabinet to be here. But the Navy's not an easy post tonight.—Is that all?

FOLWELL. Yes, Mr. President.

GORDON. Well, Bob, suppose you escort Miss Folwell downstairs.

ROBERT. Yes, Father. [*Goes to her and offers his arm.*] Miss Folwell, may I have the pleasure?

FOLWELL. Thank you!

GORDON [*to* FOLWELL]. Perhaps you will speak to Mrs. Gordon on your way down. Tell her it's about time for us to join the party.

ROBERT. We'll tell her, Dad.—You first, Miss Folwell. [*Exit* FOLWELL *and* ROBERT.]

DUNCAN. I brought along some press clippings from the evening papers, Mr. President. If you have time to see them. [GORDON *takes clippings.*]

GORDON. Reports on the inaugural address?

DUNCAN. Yes, Mr. President.

GORDON. We're here for four years, Duncan. "Sir" will do, if you insist.—What do they say?

DUNCAN. None of them very helpful, if I may summarize.

GORDON [*smiles*]. Did you expect them to be?

DUNCAN. No, sir.

GORDON. [*Goes to table and puts down clippings. Turns to fireplace, front.*] What did *you* think of my speech, Duncan?

DUNCAN [*laughs*]. After all . . .

GORDON. I know, you helped me prepare it. . . .

DUNCAN. Not the speech you made, sir.—Shall I tell you what I was thinking of, while you spoke?

GORDON. Please!

DUNCAN. There is really no such thing as eloquence.—It's belief that people want.—When that war-crazy mob began finally to listen, I said to myself: "They'll always listen to a man who *believes* what he says."

GORDON. [*Goes to* DUNCAN, *holds out his hand.*] Thank you, Duncan.—This is the first time today I've shaken hands with a man because I *wanted* to.

[*Enter* MRS. GORDON, *a lovely, quiet woman of about thirty-five or forty years. Goes to desk and puts down corsage.*]

MRS. GORDON. Are you ready, dear?

GORDON. Yes, my dear, of course. We've just settled a great problem.

MRS. GORDON. [*Goes to* GORDON *and pins his flower on.*] What problem?

GORDON. I wasn't quite sure I was President of the United States. Mr. Duncan has convinced me.

MRS. GORDON. I'm glad of that. [*To* DUNCAN.] Thank you, Mr. Duncan.

DUNCAN. You're looking very beautiful, Mrs. Gordon. Do you mind my saying so?

MRS. GORDON. [*Turns* GORDON *around; looks at him.*] No, I like it! How long have we before the President's March? [*Goes to table; pins on flowers.*]

DUNCAN. [*Consults watch.*] Exactly . . . three and one-half minutes!

MRS. GORDON. You're very exact. Did I interrupt anything?

GORDON. No, dear.

DUNCAN. There *is* one thing else, sir. I didn't want to worry you, tonight, but you're bound to hear it, downstairs.

GORDON. Well. . . .

DUNCAN. Senator Bright called up. He had a statement to make.

GORDON. Oh, Massachusetts wants war!

DUNCAN. Yes, sir. But what he really called up to say was that Mr. Fitzgerald and Mr. Wilmot have organized a committee of Congressmen to wait on you tomorrow morning before the Cabinet meeting.

GORDON. Oh! Did he mention why?

DUNCAN. I believe to inform you that Congress intends to declare war, at the session tomorrow.

GORDON. So we've got to face that issue at once.

Very well, Duncan. Make the appointment. And by the way, try not to let anything interrupt the function tonight.

DUNCAN. I understand, sir. [*To* MRS. GORDON.] Excuse me. [*He smiles. Exits.*]

MRS. GORDON. [*After pause, goes to* GORDON.] Mr. President. [*Kisses* GORDON.]

GORDON. Three minutes and a half.

MRS. GORDON. Less, by now.

GORDON. Are you frightened?

MRS. GORDON. Are you?

GORDON. [*Smiles, turns to her.*] I feel rather like the king in the story, who went down naked to the great hall. All the courtiers bowed down and agreed that the king was very handsome in his purple and fine linen.—All but one!—I wonder who he will be?

MRS. GORDON. [*Fixes corsage.*] Why, that's the story I used to read to Robert.

GORDON. I never thought it would come true—about *me*.

MRS. GORDON. It hasn't come true about you.

GORDON. I haven't had such a funny feeling since the Illinois strike.

MRS. GORDON. [*Takes his hand.*] The strike at Gerson? You told me you were never worried for a minute!

GORDON. I wasn't!—But I did think, along about

the third day, that I might be comforted by the sight of a gun.

MRS. GORDON. It would have made thinks *look* safer.—I'm glad you didn't call out the militia. I know how you feel. I have the same feeling too. It passes.

[*Music: "Hail to the Chief."* GORDON *goes to desk, gets handkerchief, then to door, opens it, and back to* MRS. GORDON.]

GORDON. Well, here we go.

MRS. GORDON. [*Stopping a moment, and solemnly to* GORDON.] I know, whatever happens tonight —you'll do what you know is right.

GORDON. If I only knew what that was.

MRS. GORDON. You always have before.—Don't you, now?

GORDON. [*Pause.*] Mrs. President, I haven't the least idea! [*They start out together.*]

CURTAIN

SCENE III

[*The White House. A small room off the reception room. A few minutes before the end of Scene II.* MRS. BANE, *the Dowager, with* MANSFIELD, *the young Diplomat, the* BRITISH AMBASSADOR, *the*

FRENCH AMBASSADOR, *and* SENATOR BRIGHT, *a polished, cultured, somewhat pompous product of Boston, form a group.* SECRETARY OF STATE DICKINSON, *an elderly statesman, of fine appearance, is the center of another group. General company assembled awaiting the arrival of the* PRESIDENT. *Music.*]

MANSFIELD. My God! Here comes Mrs. Bane. Hide me!

MRS. BANE. Good evening, Mr. Ambassador.

BRITISH AMBASSADOR. Good evening, Mrs. Bane.

MRS. BANE. Lovely party, isn't it? I hope you're coming to mine next Wednesday.

BRITISH AMBASSADOR. Thank you. I received your invitation.

MRS. BANE. Oh, Ambassador Giradaut.

FRENCH AMBASSADOR. Mrs. Bane.

MRS. BANE. Where is your fascinating wife?

FRENCH AMBASSADOR. She's here, Madame.

MRS. BANE. Oh, what a pity! such competition! Ah! Mr. Mansfield, the baby of the State Department. You're going to dance with me, young man.

MANSFIELD. I suppose . . . I mean thank you, Mrs. Bane.

MRS. BANE [*To* FRENCH AMBASSADOR.] Oh!

Excellency, I understand the Japanese Ambassador hasn't come.

FRENCH AMBASSADOR. You do not say, Madame.

MRS. BANE. Does that mean he isn't coming?

MANSFIELD. I think he will be here, Mrs. Bane, the evening is young.

MRS. BANE. But he shouldn't be late. It's rather significant, isn't it? What do you think, Senator Bright?

BRIGHT. I beg your pardon, Mrs. Bane.

MRS. BANE. Shouldn't the Japanese Ambassador be here with the other ambassadors?

BRIGHT. The Japanese have a most delicate sense of courtesy. Perhaps his Excellency thought that his absence would be more welcome than his presence.

MRS. BANE. Oh, you discreet New Englanders! [*Catches sight of* DICKINSON, *addresses him.*] Well, here's the Secretary of State, perhaps he can inform us. Good evening, Mr. Dickinson.

DICKINSON. Good evening, Mrs. Bane.

MRS. BANE. Good evening, Mrs. Dickinson. I've always admired that dress. Now tell me, Mr. Secretary, ex-officially, isn't it strange that the Japanese Ambassador isn't here?

DICKINSON. I hadn't thought of it, Mrs. Bane. But there are other ambassadors to lend dignity to our party.

MRS. BANE. Oh, yes. Dignity, but not excitement. Everyone's being so tactful, aren't they?

[*The President's March is heard.*]

MRS. BANE. Ah, the President's March. We must go in! Now where's my young man? Ah, there you are; you may have the honor.

[*Exit* MRS. BANE *and* MANSFIELD.]

DICKINSON [*to* BRIGHT]. Are you coming, Mr. Senator?

BRIGHT. After you, Mr. Secretary. Even Massachusetts can't precede the Department of State. [DICKINSON *exits.* BRIGHT *is about to follow, when he is stopped by the entrance of* FITZGERALD, *a blatant, somewhat vulgar politician of the patrioteer type.*]

FITZGERALD. [*Takes* BRIGHT'S *hand and shakes it.*] Senator Bright, have you talked to the President?

BRIGHT. No, Mr. Fitzgerald. But I've made the appointment for tomorrow morning.

FITZGERALD. Can you imagine a reception in the White House, with the country in a state of war!

BRIGHT. Not quite at war yet, Mr. Representative.

FITZGERALD. With the army mobilizing and the fleet at sea? Is there nothing we can do but dance?

BRIGHT. Well, really, Mr. Fitzgerald. It's only proper that we should complete the inauguration.

FITZGERALD. That pig-headed pacifist in the presidential chair tonight!

BRIGHT. You're speaking of President Gordon.

FITZGERALD. Sorry. But he's dangerous. Who knows what will happen? [*Enter* SENATOR HILL, *of California, well-groomed, courteous, cynical, and* REPRESENTATIVE SMITH, *of Georgia, a kindly, soft-spoken gentleman, well-intentioned but weak.*] Senator Hill, how do you do?

HILL. Good evening, Mr. Fitzgerald. You remember Mr. Smith?

FITZGERALD. I make it my business, Mr. Smith! [*Shakes* SMITH'S *hand, much to his annoyance.*] You know Senator Bright.

BRIGHT. It's a pleasure to see you, Mr. Representative. You're from Georgia, aren't you? My family used to own . . . [*They talk together.*]

FITZGERALD [*aside to* HILL]. Well, did you get a fifth man for our committee?

HILL. Smith has agreed to serve if we can assure him we won't force the President's hand.

FITZGERALD. Smith. That mollycoddle!

HILL. Smith is from Georgia. If we are going to insist on war, the South has got to be represented on the committee.

FITZGERALD [*looking at* SMITH]. The man's dangerous to us. He carried twelve southern votes against the munitions bill last fall.

HILL. We've got time before tomorrow to attend to Mr. Smith's southern votes. At any rate I guess we can out-talk him in committee.

FITZGERALD [*leaving* HILL, *goes to* SMITH]. Well, Mr. Representative. You're going to serve on our committee. Good. [*Shakes his hand.*]

SMITH. I wish we could have a referendum, instead of a committee.

FITZGERALD. Referendum?

SMITH. I resent the way the Congress is threatening to stand between President Gordon and the people who elected him. Of course, a referendum is absurd to hope for. That's why I'm accepting the post on your committee.

BRIGHT. We organized this committee, Mr. Smith, with the express idea of being perfectly fair with the President. We realize, of course, that war is inevitable, but we want to understand the President's mind, and find out any possible way of cooperating with him. Of course, like Mr. Fitzgerald, I would like to see action.

FITZGERALD. Action is what we need. Now if we could find some quiet room where we can discuss our plan of attack. . . .

[TURNER *enters, passing through.*]

BRIGHT. Oh, Turner, we have something for you.

TURNER. Good evening, gentlemen.—That statement of yours is all fixed, Senator Bright.

Massachusetts wants war. See you later. [*He starts off.*]

BRIGHT. I have something to add.

TURNER. Some reference to Lincoln? Oh, I've got Lincoln in, Senator. I never forget Lincoln.

BRIGHT. No. No. This is . . .

FITZGERALD. What he wants to tell you is that Mr. Smith of Georgia has consented to serve as the fifth member of our committee.

TURNER. Mr. Smith is fifth—I see. Thanks, gentlemen. [*Writes down name.*] Anything else, give to Mr. Duncan, will you? He's free. I've got to go and greet the President. Aren't you gentlemen coming?

FITZGERALD. In a minute.

TURNER. O.K.

[*Exit* TURNER. SMITH *starts to leave, as his wife enters.*]

SMITH [*to wife*]. Hello, dear.—If you'll excuse me, gentlemen, I'll join the receiving line. You see, I've never met the President, nor his wife. I'd like to. [*Exit* SMITH *and his wife.*]

FITZGERALD. Why the hell do you want Smith on the committee?

HILL. I told you. He's protective coloration.

FITZGERALD. Protective what?

BRIGHT. [*Laughs.*] This is only your second Congress, Fitzgerald. Even in an emergency, we mustn't forget *tactics* are necessary to win points.

[*Enter* SECRETARY FULTON, *a dignified, friendly man, showing signs of mental strain.*]

HILL. Good evening, Mr. Fulton.

BRIGHT. Good evening. What's the news from the War Department?

FULTON. Good evening.—Possibly you know more about it than I do. Well, shall we go in? Mr. Bright, Mr. Hill?

FITZGERALD. Oh, Mr. Fulton! So the Secretary of War has time to dance tonight. I haven't noticed the Secretary of the Navy here.

FULTON. Mr. Aldrich is probably busy at the Navy Department. I'm busy myself, but I thought, since I'd been invited, I'd pay my respects to the President.

FITZGERALD. Perhaps the War Department would like to know that we have formed a committee to wait on the President tomorrow morning, to represent Congress. Senator Bright is chairman.

FULTON. The Cabinet meets at two, Mr. Bright.

BRIGHT. Of course, Fulton. This will be just a preliminary talk——

FULTON. [*Pauses, as he faces them.*] I see. To continue Brainard's administration?

FITZGERALD. Congress is the body empowered to declare war.

FULTON. Let's have this straight, gentlemen. I'm with President Gordon. All the way. Every step, and further.—If you intend to block his path, then—count me out.

[*Enter* DICKINSON, SECRETARY OF STATE, *maintaining the amenities of the occasion.*]

DICKINSON. Mr. Fulton . . . ! [FULTON *stops.*] I understand there's a messenger here looking for you.

FULTON. Thank you, sir. I'll find him at once. [*Exits.*]

DICKINSON. The President is receiving, gentlemen. Have you been in?

BRIGHT. We're just about to go in.

DICKINSON. [*Shaking hands with* HILL.] I hear there's *one* charming lady present, Mr. Hill—from Sacramento. . . .

HILL. [*Softening, under the tone of* DICKINSON.] I hope you mean Mrs. Hill?

DICKINSON. I've never had the pleasure.—Mr. Fitzgerald, is Mrs. Fitzgerald with you?

FITZGERALD. *No,* sir! I came alone.

DICKINSON. Then why don't you let me introduce you to some fine specimens of the Old World Aristocracy. They're *all* here, eager to see what the President means by dancing on the drums. I think he's splendid. Don't you?

[FITZGERALD *is silenced. He follows* DICKINSON *down the corridor with* HILL. DICKINSON *and* HILL *are about to exit when* REPRESENTATIVE WILMOT *enters. He is a formidable figure, tall, arrogant, the business man in politics. He goes to* DICKINSON.]

WILMOT. Good evening, Mr. Secretary!

DICKINSON. Mr. Wilmot, good evening.

WILMOT. I would like to see the President, at once.

DICKINSON. He is busy receiving his guests.

WILMOT. How long is this nonsense going on? I've got some business to talk about.

DICKINSON. I'm afraid you'll have to wait, Mr. Wilmot. Let's go in to the reception.

WILMOT. Oh, I'm out of sympathy with this damned reception.

[MRS. WILMOT *and* MRS. HILL *enter.—Ad lib. introductions.* FULTON *enters, followed by* MESSENGER.]

FULTON. Oh, Mr. Secretary.

DICKINSON. Yes, Mr. Fulton.

FULTON. [*Agitated, holding message.*] A dispatch has just come through. I'm on my way to verify it. I may have to see Mr. Gordon alone.

DICKINSON [*jovially*]. Surely your news can wait. We can't interrupt the reception line.

FULTON. If this dispatch is correct, I shall have to see the President at once.

MESSENGER. Mr. Fulton, sir?

[FULTON *signs messenger's book, after which exit* MESSENGER.]

FITZGERALD. Fulton, what are you keeping from us?

BRIGHT. Possibly it's none of our business, Mr. Representative!

FITZGERALD. Maybe not yours, Mr. Senator, but *I* promised the voters of the sovereign State of Wyoming . . .

DICKINSON. Let's not worry about campaign promises tonight. Come along. . . . You know, I'd forgotten Wyoming was a state, hadn't you, Hill?

[*Exit* HILL, DICKINSON, FITZGERALD, *after them* BRIGHT.]

WILMOT. What is your important news, Mr. Secretary?

FULTON [*quietly*]. You will no doubt learn it tomorrow.

WILMOT. That may be too late.—I have reasons for wanting to know it tonight.

FULTON. My message is for the President. I happen to be his Secretary of War.

WILMOT. Congratulations! I am Chairman of the House Military Affairs Committee. What keeps you from relaying important news?

FULTON. Something you could not possibly understand. You and Brainard between you have done everything you could to force Gordon into a war with Japan. I haven't the heart to tell him that perhaps you've *done* it.

WILMOT. So! If you have information in your possession, from the front . . .

FULTON [*letting go*]. The *front* already! I'm War Secretary, and nobody has told *me* of a Declaration of War!

WILMOT. Well, that's just a mere technical——

FULTON [*interrupting*]. President Gordon is in charge of the government tonight, Mr. Representative. If he can convince you and your crowd of that, perhaps he can still manage Japan.

WILMOT. Fight them, you mean?

FULTON. That remains for the President to decide.

WILMOT. Mr. Secretary, I insist for reasons of my own, that it is my duty to learn what is in that dispatch!

FULTON [*vigorously*]. You'll know when President Gordon chooses to tell you—and not a damned minute before!

[FULTON *storms out.* WILMOT *withdraws rear,*

as guests begin to return from reception room, led by BRIGHT, FITZGERALD, TURNER, DUNCAN, *etc.*]

FITZGERALD. That's enough for me! What do you say, Wilmot, let's go?

DUNCAN [*drily*]. Better stay around for the excitement.

TURNER. What excitement?—You know something you haven't told me?

DUNCAN. There's bound to be a break for you this evening. Maybe the fleet's been sunk.

FITZGERALD. If that's your idea of a joke, Duncan . . . ! [*Starts off.*]

TURNER. Don't go, Fitzgerald. We're counting on you for a story.

FITZGERALD. You'll have plenty of story tomorrow after the committee meeting.

DUNCAN. You always do your duty by the press, Mr. Fitzgerald. See if you can get us a nice big war.

[FITZGERALD *leaves them huffily, and crosses up to* WILMOT.]

DUNCAN [*to* TURNER]. Maybe Wilmot can give you a headline about munitions, Turner. He's been swelling like a blow-fish all evening.

TURNER. I've *got* Representative Wilmot's story. I'm saving it.

DUNCAN. For the investigation?

TURNER. For my autobiography. The low-down on that gunpowder-king and his war lobby is going to pay for my old age, and plenty!

[*Enter* MISS FOLWELL.]

DUNCAN. Hello, Folwell, you're looking wiser than usual.

FOLWELL. Don't look now—that was an earl I just left. He couldn't quite place me here, but he thinks I'm Mata Hari.

DUNCAN. Couldn't he tell a working-girl's hands? [*She shows them.*] They don't show signs of labor. What do you use?

FOLWELL. I sit on them.

DUNCAN [*starting off with* MISS FOLWELL]. See you later, Turner.

TURNER. No, you don't. This is my only dance this evening.

DUNCAN [*to* MISS FOLWELL]. Why are you wasting your dance on Turner?

FOLWELL. It's an election bet.

TURNER. And she won!

FOLWELL. No, I lost!

TURNER [*laughing*]. What this country needs is more Folwells. [*He dances off with her.*]

WILMOT. Duncan, Mr. Fulton is looking for the President!

DUNCAN. Is that so? What for?

[HILL, MRS. HILL, MANSFIELD, MRS. BANE *enter.*]

WILMOT. That's what I want to know.

DUNCAN. It's just as well not to know too much tonight, Mr. Wilmot. There are plenty of rumors around. Fortunately the government doesn't proceed on rumor.

MRS. BANE. Rumor? Have you heard something, Mr. Wilmot?

MR. WILMOT. Unfortunately not, Mrs. Bane.

MRS. BANE. Some strange stories are coming through from California.

HILL. From California?

MRS. BANE. Oh, yes. I have heard that Admiral James has just been informed that there is a Japanese submarine base right in San Francisco harbor.

HILL. I didn't notice one when I left.

MRS. BANE. Oh, but I'm quite sure it's true.

[HILL *and* MRS. HILL *turn, then exit.*]

MANSFIELD. And that isn't the worst of it, Mrs. Bane. Have you heard about the shipment of Japanese beetles they found on the docks of the Dollar Line?

MRS. BANE. Japanese beetles!

WILMOT. Beetles, Mrs. Bane! It's guns we have got to worry about. We've got a war on our hands.

MRS. BANE. Isn't it exciting! But Mr. Mansfield is in the State Department, and he assures me it won't come right away.

MANSFIELD. I think I said, Mrs. Bane, that I

hoped it wouldn't come at all. Will you excuse me, I have the next dance with Miss Folwell?

[*Exit* MANSFIELD *and* MISS FOLWELL.]

MRS. BANE. If you gentlemen wanted to be sure of a war, you should have been careful to elect a war President.

BRIGHT. So you really think the President will keep us out of it?

[DICKINSON, BRITISH AMBASSADOR, FRENCH AMBASSADOR *enter.*]

MRS. BANE. Oh, he must for a while. Anyhow, I've sent out invitations for my dinner next Wednesday.

WILMOT. We must wait for that anyway.

[MRS. BANE, BRIGHT, WILMOT *exit.*]

SECRETARY DICKINSON. [*Talking to a group of ambassadors.*] Yes, I met Lord Carrington during the war. He entertained us at headquarters with stories of Tokio.

BRITISH AMBASSADOR. He's the oldest member of the Foreign Office. I served under him as Chargé for two years. He should be very helpful to you in the event of trouble.

FRENCH AMBASSADOR. Great Britain is always in a position to be helpful, in the Orient. Paris has counted on her more than once.

SECRETARY DICKINSON. We shall have to count on her directly, if I'm not mistaken.

BRITISH AMBASSADOR. You're pessimistic, Mr. Secretary. Our War Office has great confidence in your miracle-man, President Gordon.

FRENCH AMBASSADOR. Perhaps your War Office has more confidence in Britain's Grand Fleet.—In France, we think in terms of borders. When one can see the enemy across a river, one does not count on miracles.

SECRETARY DICKINSON. [*Smiles.*] I believe you.—America has learned to be grateful for the Pacific Ocean. But it's not as wide as it once was.

[MANSFIELD *enters with* MISS FOLWELL. *They join the group, with greetings.*]

FOLWELL. Good evening.

DICKINSON. Good evening, Miss Folwell. [*To* MANSFIELD.] You've been in the Department of State for two years, my boy. Why don't *you* tell us who can settle the mess?

MANSFIELD. [*Laughs.*] Thank you, Mr. Secretary, but that's rather unfair.

DICKINSON. Not at all—is it, Miss Folwell?

FOLWELL. Well, it's a bit severe.

DICKINSON. I'm an old-timer. *He's* one of the boys who will have to fight.

FOLWELL. No one will have to fight!

MANSFIELD. At any rate, I shan't. I'm in the diplomatic service. But I don't want war.

BRITISH AMBASSADOR. I should hope not. It's so *final.*

DICKINSON. Yes, very final.

MANSFIELD. And, in the case of Japan, so unfortunate. Don't you think?

DICKINSON. That's rather a bold opinion, just now.

MANSFIELD. It is, sir. But you see, I have been to Japan, and seen the people. I think I understand the peace movement of . . . Koyé.

FRENCH AMBASSADOR. Koyé? He's got quite a reputation in Tokio.

BRITISH AMBASSADOR. Lord Carrington calls him "the Emperor of the People."

DICKINSON. Of course I have known of Koyé for years. I've never met him, but——

MANSFIELD. Oh, but you have, sir. Five years ago at a peace lecture at Columbia University, when I was an undergraduate. Koyé had come to this country to study labor conditions, and he was asked to speak after you finished.

DICKINSON [*meditatively*]. Of course, that was Koyé! I had forgotten.

MANSFIELD. I haven't, Mr. Secretary. Koyé made a deep impression on me that night.

FRENCH AMBASSADOR. That's amusing—the man to save you has been trained right here in your own country!

FOLWELL. Yes, we have good ideas in America—but we give them away.

MANSFIELD. When I traveled in the East, before entering the service, I met him in Japan. He lives in the slums of Tokio.

BRITISH AMBASSADOR. Yes, he has considerable influence with labor.

MANSFIELD. Yes, sir. He is also very popular in the universities. Crowds are with him everywhere.

BRITISH AMBASSADOR. For something like twenty years, Koyé has been organizing the people, the common people, of Japan.

MANSFIELD. Yes, sir, organizing them for peace.

DICKINSON. Peace? We aren't hearing much of it now.

MANSFIELD. It's there, sir. That's the reason why General Nogatu has been rushing his country into war. The Government is afraid that Koyé will force their hand.

FRENCH AMBASSADOR. That's what a military dictatorship always has to do.

MANSFIELD. Provoke a war abroad when there's trouble at home.

DICKINSON. Well, that's very interesting, Mansfield.

FOLWELL. Yes, he's quite a statesman, and a very fine dancer.

MANSFIELD. I thank you, sir. [*Exit* MANSFIELD *with* MISS FOLWELL.]

[*Enter* WILMOT *and* MRS. WILMOT.]

WILMOT [*to* FITZGERALD]. Fitzgerald! Have you heard about the Jennings Steel contracts?

FITZGERALD. What about them?

WILMOT. Canceled, this afternoon. By executive order.

FITZGERALD. Canceled? You must be crazy!

WILMOT. Do you know who's crazy? Gordon! I'm going to take the first chance I get to tell him so. Where does he think his money support's coming from? School-children?

FITZGERALD. Tell him tomorrow in committee.

WILMOT. Tomorrow! Jennings makes guns! You can't hold up Jennings like a God-damn store-keeper!

[*Enter* GORDON, MRS. GORDON, ROBERT, *and* DUNCAN. MRS. BANE *and* BRIGHT *follow.*]

MRS. GORDON. You can stop smiling, dear, if you want to.

GORDON. You're mistaken. It's permanent. I've done nothing since this morning but smile.

ROBERT [*showing a button, in his hand*]. Dad, look what the British Ambassador gave me!

MRS. GORDON. That's awfully kind of you, Sir Guy.

BRITISH AMBASSADOR. Delighted.

GORDON. You'd better look out for your medals, Mr. Ambassador.

MRS. GORDON. I do think Robert should be off to bed. It's so late.

GORDON. Let him have a good time.

[*Enter* TURNER, *joins the group.*]

TURNER. Excuse me for breaking into a family conference, Mrs. Gordon.

MRS. GORDON. Not at all, Mr. Turner. While you're here we all feel safe.

TURNER. I just wanted to make my excuses. I have to leave.

GORDON. Oh, I'm sorry. Anything important?

TURNER. Just to call the city editors.

DUNCAN. Mr. Turner has to deny another rumor.

GORDON. What rumor?

TURNER. Number three hundred and sixty-seven, sir. That the Japanese have a submarine base in San Francisco.

GORDON. Who started that ridiculous story? But there are plenty of people who'll believe it, I suppose.—Deny it, by all means.

TURNER [*disgustedly*]. It's almost too silly.

GORDON. Deny it, I say. Kill it. And any other lie! Facts are what we want.

TURNER [*vehemently*]. If I could get hold of a *fact* tonight, Mr. President . . . I'd get the Pulitzer Prize by unanimous vote.

[*Exit* TURNER. MRS. BANE *approaches.*]

MRS. GORDON. [*Quickly, to* DUNCAN.] Please, who is that, Mr. Duncan . . . ?

DUNCAN. Mrs. Bane, the Dowager Empress.

MRS. GORDON. A thousand thanks.

[GORDON *leaves them, with* DUNCAN.]

MRS. BANE [*to* MRS. GORDON]. Oh, Mrs. Gordon, *such* a lovely reception!

MRS. GORDON. Mrs. Bane, how nice of you to stay.

MRS. BANE. I wouldn't miss a minute of it for the *world*. [*Drawing* MRS. GORDON *aside*.] Have you talked to Mrs. Wilmot?

MRS. GORDON. I haven't had the opportunity. Why?

MRS. BANE. She's such an innocent soul. She told me, just now—you mustn't repeat a word of this——

MRS. GORDON. Oh, now, Mrs. Bane, please!—You mustn't ask me to keep state secrets. Remember, this is my first encounter with Washington. [MRS. BANE *speaks to her, aside, then they rejoin the group.* MRS. BANE *exits.*]

DICKINSON. [*To* PRESIDENT GORDON, *with whom he has been speaking, away from the others.*] I should think you'd be all in.

GORDON. It's pure bluff, Dickinson.—Good evening, Mr. Wilmot.

WILMOT. [*Joining them.*] Mr. President. If I might speak with you privately.

GORDON. That's not quite convenient, Mr. Wilmot. What is it?

DICKINSON. Don't mind me. I'm going.

GORDON. Not at all necessary.—Mr. Wilmot, do you think we need discuss contracts tonight?

WILMOT. Contracts? I didn't mention contracts.

GORDON. No, but you were going to.

WILMOT. All right! Why did you cancel the Jennings Steel contracts?

GORDON. Because it was part of the scheme to force the country into war. And, incidentally, they were very bad contracts.

[MRS. GORDON *joins* MRS. WILMOT.]

WILMOT. They were recommended by a Congressional committee!

GORDON. This is inauguration day, Mr. Wilmot! —And this happens to be a social occasion. Please let it go on!

WILMOT. Is that a refusal to consider——

GORDON. It is a request from the Executive to confine business matters to business hours. Don't forget, Wilmot, that I have helped run other companies besides the United States of America. There's a difference, and I'd like to observe it.

FITZGERALD. [*Comes down, to* WILMOT.] Tomorrow, Wilmot! Remember where you are!

WILMOT. I *know* where I am. In the White House.

GORDON. Then please don't confuse it with the lobbies of the Capitol!

[GORDON *exits with* DICKINSON.]

MRS. GORDON. Oh, Mr. Wilmot. I haven't had the opportunity to talk to you.

MR. WILMOT. That is my misfortune, Mrs. Gordon.

MRS. GORDON. I've just had a chat with your wife.

ROBERT [*showing another button to his mother*]. Oh, Mother, look what the French Ambassador gave me.

MRS. GORDON. Listen, dear, you mustn't go around collecting buttons. Oh, Mr. Wilmot, may I present you to the French Ambassador, Monsieur Giradaut. This is Mr. Wilmot, Representative from Illinois.

[FULTON *enters hurriedly. Goes to* DUNCAN.]

FULTON. Oh, Mr. Duncan.

DUNCAN. Yes, Mr. Fulton?

[*Enter* MRS. BANE.]

MRS. BANE. Ah! Mr. Fulton.

FULTON. Excuse me, Mrs. Bane. [*To* DUNCAN.] I must see the President.

DUNCAN. He has asked me not to interfere with the function.

FULTON. I have a message that can't wait.

DUNCAN. Very good, sir. I'll find him. Excuse me, Mrs. Bane.

MRS. BANE. Something for the President that can't wait?

FULTON. Yes, Mrs. Bane. Excuse me!

[MISS FOLWELL *and* MANSFIELD *enter.* MISS FOLWELL *meets* DUNCAN.]

FOLWELL. Hey, why haven't you asked me to dance?

DUNCAN. Where is the President?

FOLWELL. In the ballroom. What's up?

DUNCAN. Fulton's got a message. [*Exits.*]

MRS. BANE [*to* MISS FOLWELL]. There's a message for the President that can't wait.

FOLWELL. Is that so, Mrs. Bane?

[MRS. BANE *rushes over to a General.*]

MRS. BANE. Oh, General. I know you know what's going on, so don't pretend——

[FOLWELL *crosses to* MRS. GORDON.]

MRS. GORDON. Is Mr. Duncan looking for John?

FOLWELL. Yes, Mrs. Gordon. [*Turns to* MANSFIELD.] Go and dance with Mrs. Bane.

MANSFIELD. Oh, Mrs. Bane, may I have this dance?

MRS. BANE. [*Spying* MR. FITZGERALD.] Have you heard, Mr. Fitzgerald? News for the President.

[SENATOR HILL *and* MRS. HILL *enter.*]

FITZGERALD. No, Mrs. Bane. We Congressmen are told nothing.

MANSFIELD. This dance, Mrs. Bane!

MRS. BANE. Dance! Don't be silly. Oh, Mr. Hill—it must be something from California.

HILL. What, Mrs. Bane?

MRS. BANE. Mr. Fulton has a message. It's those Jap submarines.

MANSFIELD. This dance, Mrs. Bane!

MRS. BANE. Yes, but here comes the President.

[GORDON *and* DUNCAN *enter and go direct to* FULTON.]

GORDON. You have a message for me? Thank you, Fulton. I'll take it here. What does it say?

FULTON. I'd rather hand it to you in private.

GORDON. But there's no need for secrecy. I'll take it here.

[FULTON *hesitates. Others watch. He hands* GORDON *cable.* GORDON *reads quickly. He is stunned. Pause.*]

GORDON. How did this come through?

FULTON. By cable from Shanghai. . . . Before the wires were destroyed.

GORDON. Did you verify it?

FULTON. Yes, sir. Through the War Department radio station. I have just come from there.

GORDON. [*Looks at message, then at room. Eyes meet* MRS. GORDON. GORDON *goes with* FULTON, *talking as they go out.*] They must have given orders to their fleet days ago.

FULTON. Yes. Before they sent the reply to the ultimatum.

GORDON. When did it happen?

FULTON. Late this afternoon.

GORDON. But how? In God's name, why? [*Exits.*]

[DUNCAN *goes to* MRS. GORDON.]

DUNCAN. Don't be worried. Go ahead with your reception. [*Exit* DUNCAN.]

MRS. GORDON. Miss Folwell, what do you suppose has happened?

FOLWELL. I'll go and find out for you.

MRS. GORDON. Go speak to that orchestra first, please. Keep them dancing.

[*Exit* MISS FOLWELL.]

MRS. BANE. Mr. Hill, do you know what has happened?

HILL. I'm bound to say I don't, Mrs. Bane.

[TURNER *enters, crosses the stage hurriedly.*]

HILL. Oh, Mr. Turner.

TURNER. Not just now, Mr. Hill. You must excuse me.

MRS. GORDON. Mr. Turner.

TURNER. [*Stops, then crosses to her.*] Yes, Mrs. Gordon?

MRS. GORDON. A dispatch just came through. Do you know what it was?

TURNER. Yes. An official dispatch. Japan has taken Manila.

MRS. GORDON [*frightened, and incredulous*]. Japan has taken Manila!

FITZGERALD [*who has overheard, in loud voice*]. Japan has taken Manila.

[*The company takes up the announcement, which spreads throughout the room. Great excitement and confusion. A babel of voices.*]

CURTAIN

SCENE IV

[*The* PRESIDENT'S *room in the White House. Evening of Inauguration Day, just after close of Scene III.* GORDON *and* FULTON *face each other across the room. The* PRESIDENT *is sitting at his desk, with message in his hand.* MUSIC, *soft, during scene.*]

FULTON. That's all I know—what's there, in the cable. Admiral James tells me they must have forced the harbor in a surprise attack by seaplanes, fired on the city, landed. . . .

GORDON. What were our losses?

FULTON. There are no figures. You know what it means, John—we can't avoid war. This settles it.

GORDON. I can't think that.

FULTON. What escape is there?

GORDON. We're old friends, George. We think the same way. . . .

FULTON. We always have.—But we have no choice now, as members of the Government. Japan's defied us.

GORDON. [*Breaking out.*] She's defied Brainard's ultimatum! Why? Because it *was* an ultimatum—an unfriendly act.

FULTON. None the less, it has happened. . . .

GORDON. Why has she seized Manila?—Because the President of the United States treated her like an enemy? We shook our sword and dared her to strike. And she's struck!

FULTON. Japan has committed an act of war.

GORDON. If we *make* it one, by striking back.—Try for the millionth time to make two wrongs a right!

FULTON. There's no more time for philosophizing. . . .

GORDON. [*Pause.*] Remember what we promised each other, when we won the election last November? We knew then that Brainard was trying to stir up a war. . . .

FULTON. I never imagined it would come to firing on our flag!

GORDON. That lays a command on both of us. To

stick to our promises! I'm going to. Are you? [DUNCAN *enters.*] What is it, Duncan?

DUNCAN. The Secretary of the Navy to see you, sir.

GORDON. Show him in.

DUNCAN. Yes, Mr. President. [*Exit* DUNCAN.]

FULTON. You'll want to see Aldrich alone. [*Starts to go.*]

GORDON. [*Rises.*] Aren't the Army and Navy speaking? I wish you'd stay.

[FULTON *looks at* GORDON. *There is a moment of hesitation.*]

FULTON. Very well.

[*Enter* DUNCAN, *followed by* ALDRICH, *Secretary of the Navy. A straight, athletic type, with the manner of a man used to commanding attention.*]

DUNCAN. The Secretary of the Navy, sir. [*Exits.*]

FULTON. Good evening, Aldrich.

ALDRICH. You're here, Fulton.—Good! Then the President's *heard* the news!

GORDON. Yes. . . . We missed you this evening, Aldrich.

ALDRICH [*abruptly and excitedly*]. I have the latest dispatches. Would you like to hear them?

GORDON. [*Pause.*] If you please.

ALDRICH. Three of our destroyers sunk under enemy fire. Estimated loss on sea and land—

sailors and marines—not less than a thousand men.

FULTON. A thousand men?

ALDRICH. The Japanese hold Manila at this moment. Unless we act tonight . . .

GORDON. Tonight!

ALDRICH. We've not an hour to waste.

GORDON. Are we carrying on under Brainard?—We won't move the fleet into action tonight.

FULTON. Gordon, there's no more question. A thousand casualties . . . !

GORDON. And tomorrow ten thousand, a hundred thousand . . . ? [*To* ALDRICH.] Is this a Navy dispatch, Aldrich?

ALDRICH. Through our San Pedro station. But you can't keep such a thing quiet.

GORDON. I don't want to.

ALDRICH. [*Looks to* GORDON, *then to* FULTON.] Fulton, I'm Navy Secretary by Gordon's own appointment. I have a duty to my office, as you have . . .

GORDON. As *I* have.—I haven't forgotten that, Aldrich.

ALDRICH. We all have a duty to the people.

GORDON. [*Facing them both.*] Yes. They're going to have a *chance*.

FULTON. What chance?

GORDON. To make peace, instead of war.

ALDRICH. To make peace! [*Hands report to* GORDON.] Would you like to see the exact words, Mr. President, which tell us we have been attacked by the enemy, our soldiers shot, drowned, murdered?

GORDON. There's still a way.

ALDRICH [*impatiently*]. And what about Japan? Will she wait until we find this way . . . to peace?

GORDON. Japan wants it as much as we do.

FULTON. *We* sent the ultimatum.

GORDON. Brainard sent it. I'm not doing business on those terms.

ALDRICH. You can't help it! Good God, man, *I* believe in peace . . . !

GORDON. *Do you!*—Aldrich? No, you deceive yourself. [*Angrily.*] I'd rather hear an honest man say honestly that he believes in war, that he likes war, that a good blood-letting now and then is healthy for the world, than to hear a man like you say he believes in peace, and then, when the first chance comes to make his words good, raise his voice for war! No hypocrisy, Aldrich. We haven't time for *that,* if you please.

ALDRICH. Gordon, I've been with you all along. I stayed by when Campbell was attacked in Tokio. I agreed that one act, however violent, was not cause enough for war.—But Manila! I'm damned if I can take that lying down!

GORDON. Are you with me, or not? That's all that matters now!

ALDRICH. I'd like to be. But for God's sake, Gordon, don't make a fool of yourself and us too. Don't you suppose Brainard knew what he had to do . . .

GORDON. *Damn* Brainard! [*Pause.*] Well, at least you've made yourself clear. You and Fulton are closer to me than any men in my Cabinet. Dickinson may agree with you. I don't know. But one thing I *do* know . . .

ALDRICH. Then will you please tell us what it is? What have you planned to do? What are you going to do, *tonight?*

GORDON. [*Goes to telephone, after pause.*] Ask Mr. Duncan to come in, please?

FULTON. John, why don't you wait until the Cabinet meeting tomorrow, before making any decision?

GORDON. I have no decision to make. You've both shown me that.

ALDRICH. [*Reassured.*] I'm glad you've realized that, Gordon. We can't let personal feelings enter into this, after what's happened.

[*Enter* DUNCAN.]

GORDON. Duncan, will you send some orders?

DUNCAN. Yes, sir. [*Takes out pad and pencil.*]

GORDON. To Admiral Graham, at sea, through the Navy Station: An order to return at once to San

Francisco. Every ship under his command to be in harbor tomorrow night.

FULTON. John . . . !

ALDRICH. Mr. President . . . !

DUNCAN. —"tomorrow night."

GORDON. To the Secretary of the Navy: An order to withdraw all ships in Japanese and Chinese waters to Honolulu.

ALDRICH. Mr. President, I refuse . . . !

GORDON. Have you got that?

DUNCAN. —"Honolulu."

GORDON. To the Secretary of War: An order to return all army units to their posts, and to cancel all orders for mobilization of reserve officers.

DUNCAN. Yes, sir.

FULTON. John! For God's sake!

GORDON. And an order, please, to Mr. Dickinson, Secretary of State, to send protest and regrets to Tokio, and a request for the immediate withdrawal of all Japanese forces from Manila, in the interest of peace and good will!

DUNCAN. A memorandum to the Secretary of State covering these other orders, Mr. President?

GORDON. If you will, Duncan. And release them immediately to the press through Mr. Turner.—How long will it take?

DUNCAN. Just a few minutes, sir.

GORDON. Then go at once. Have you the note from the Japanese Ambassador?

DUNCAN. Yes, sir.

GORDON. Answer it by an invitation to lunch with me, here, tomorrow after the Cabinet meeting.

DUNCAN. Yes, Mr. President. [*Exit* DUNCAN.]

[ALDRICH *goes to* GORDON, *speaking slowly.*]

ALDRICH. Mr. President. You will agree with me that this is no time for evasion. We must be frank!

GORDON. Certainly.

ALDRICH. Then I must say that, so far as my office is concerned, these orders will *not* be issued.

GORDON. [*Pause.*] Do I understand, Mr. Secretary . . . ?

ALDRICH. I refuse to recognize or obey the orders that you have just issued to the Secretary of the Navy.

GORDON. You refuse?—In that case, sir . . .

ALDRICH. [*Interrupting.*] Yes, you're right!—I'm through, and be damned to you. You're not a peace-lover, Gordon. You're a plain coward. I'm out of your Cabinet. I *resign* tonight.

FULTON. Aldrich doesn't mean that.

ALDRICH. Don't I? I resign! And tomorrow I'll tell the country why!

FULTON. You can't let him do that, Gordon!—Aldrich, you've got to think it over. . . .

ALDRICH. No, by God! It's perfectly clear now where we stand. Retreat in the face of the enemy!—I'm getting out! And if you have any pride in your office, you'll follow me.

FULTON. Wait, Aldrich. John, be reasonable. We know each other too well for this!

GORDON. Are *you* with me?

FULTON. I think you're wrong, tonight, John. But however wrong you may be, Aldrich knows as well as I do that you're no coward.

ALDRICH. I don't know anything—except that I'm through! You'll get my resignation tonight, Mr. President. To take effect at once. [*Pause.*] We've been friends for a long time. You put me in office. But you don't know what you're doing, now. I'm going to fight you, Mr. President, with everything I've got—to save the Government from your betrayal! Good-night. [*Exit* ALDRICH *abruptly.*]

FULTON. [*Goes to* GORDON.] You've got to stop this, John. [*Pause.*] His leaving will end your administration before it's begun. Join Aldrich to Brainard and you're stopped! [*Pause.*] Let me go to him? I'll make him reconsider. He'll hold off until tomorrow . . .

GORDON. No, he won't. He means it.

FULTON. He'll reconsider, John, if you will.—Hold up those orders for another day, at least.

GORDON. You all wanted me to *act.*—Now I have.

FULTON. In anger, without thinking it out! So did Aldrich.—I must go see him, right away.—Can I tell him you've decided to wait . . . ? [GORDON *is silent.* FULTON *exits.*]

[*The* PRESIDENT, *alone, is suddenly weary. From below come the strains of "Good Night, Ladies." He goes to window at back of stage and opens the curtains, showing the lighted dome of the Capitol.* ROBERT *runs into the room and goes to* GORDON.]

ROBERT. Dad!

GORDON. Bob! [*Looks at him.*]

ROBERT. Oh, Dad! Doesn't the Capitol look great, with all those lights on the dome?

GORDON. Yes.—Beautiful! The shrine of a hundred million people whom I have sworn today to serve and protect, to guard their homes and shelter their lives. The common people, all over the country. Old men and young men, fathers and mothers, boys and girls at school, little children. All in my hands, to do with them as I will! [ROBERT *looks up at him, silent.*] How can I take them into war? To be responsible for a million graves and ten million broken hearts? Another Unknown Soldier on the hill—the symbol of unnumbered dead. [*With growing sternness.*] They are all unknown soldiers, tonight, waiting for the tombs that I am asked to build. [*Draws* ROBERT *to him.*] Go to war, Bob—with millions of boys, like you, to go away and not come back? For nothing?—No! No, I can't do that.—How can anybody do it?—I've *got* to find some other way—God helping me!

[*Enter* MRS. GORDON, *quietly. She sees the two together, joins them.*]

MRS. GORDON [*softly*]. Robert, isn't it time for bed?

ROBERT. Oh, Mother, it isn't late!

GORDON [*clasping his wife and son*]. Our first night in the White House . . .

MRS. GORDON. It's been a long time coming, hasn't it?

ROBERT. You gave a great party, Mother.

MRS. GORDON. Thank you, darling.

GORDON. But I'm glad it's over.

MRS. GORDON. So am I. I didn't feel as if I lived here—until now. The three of us, again!

GORDON [*to* ROBERT]. How about saying good-night?

ROBERT. [*Kisses them.*] Good-night, Father; good-night, Mother. I've had a *swell* time. [*Exits.*]

MRS. GORDON. [*Watching him.*] I'm so glad he's not afraid of the place.—It is bigger than home. [*She turns, looks at* GORDON, *meditatively. A silence. She waits.*]

GORDON. Well, my dear, you've heard the news?

MRS. GORDON. Manila? Of course.

GORDON. Fulton and Aldrich have been here demanding war. I've refused. I've sent dispatches cancelling Brainard's orders.

MRS. GORDON. That was splendid of you, John. [*Pause.*]

GORDON. Aldrich resigned.

MRS. GORDON. Resigned . . . ! They desert you when you need them most.—Oh, well, they were bound to.

GORDON. We might as well face it.

MRS. GORDON. [*Pause.*] Listen, dear. Aldrich's resignation isn't quite the worst of it.—Mrs. Wilmot says her husband's firm has been secretly shipping artillery west for three days.

GORDON. Artillery!—They can't wait! They're so sure it's *done!*

MRS. GORDON. [*Goes to him.*] Well, they *must* wait for *you.*

GORDON. Who am I to stop it, alone?

MRS. GORDON. [*Hands on his shoulder.*] You're President.

[GORDON *smiles, looks at her.*]

GORDON. Yes, I'm beginning to realize what that means. [GORDON, *with sudden decision, goes to telephone on desk.*]

MRS. GORDON. John, what are you doing?

GORDON. I'm afraid my orders were too hasty. I

think I should have waited at least until tomorrow. [*Lifts the telephone.*] Will you ask Mr. Duncan to come in, please.

MRS. GORDON. John, you're not going to withdraw those orders?

GORDON. God knows I don't want to. They were right. But . . .

MRS. GORDON. [*Pause, then quietly.*] Oh, John. [*Starts for the door.*]

GORDON. [*Going toward her instinctively.*] No . . . Dorothy! [*She stops.*] Don't go! I need you. I've always needed you, Dorothy, but never so much as now. I'm suddenly feeling rather helpless. [*They draw close together.*] And tonight, in this mad city! . . . For twenty years I've taught and fought for peace. I've dreamed, dared to dream of this moment. In the White House! And now that I'm here, I'm stopped by this catastrophe, without a chance.

MRS. GORDON. What better chance do you want than this! You've waited twenty years. Now the crisis has come—and you're here, *in time.*

GORDON. But when I think what Brainard has done . . .

MRS. GORDON. He's done one thing for you. He's given you the chance to prove that you believe what you have said . . . John, we'd be at war tonight, if Brainard had been President one more day.

GORDON. He was in office long enough . . .

MRS. GORDON. . . . to make things ready for you, John. Here's your chance to prevent war, to make peace, to do what you have been promising and preparing to do all your life. I'm only one person who's counting on you. There are a million others, praying tonight. . . . They've got to, John. There's nothing else to do but pray for *you* . . . that you will save us all from war.

GORDON. If I could only see the way through—what to do!

MRS. GORDON. No one knows just what to do at a time like this. But it comes—it comes! It will come to you, John.

GORDON. My dear. [*Kisses her hand. Knock on door.*] Come in. [DUNCAN *enters.*] Oh—Duncan.

DUNCAN. [*Taking in the situation.*] Didn't you call me, sir?

GORDON. [*Pause.*] Have you . . . delivered those orders?

DUNCAN. Not all of them, Mr. President.—Did you want to make any change?

GORDON. [*Pause.*] No.—There is nothing to change. I'm sorry I called you.—Good-night, Duncan.

DUNCAN. Good-night, Mr. President. [*Exits.*]

CURTAIN

ACT TWO

ACT TWO

[*The White House. A private office. The next morning at ten o'clock.* GORDON *is seated at his desk.* DUNCAN *stands beside him, reading from a notebook.* GORDON *has a breakfast tray and is finishing his coffee. A band can be heard outside playing "The Star Spangled Banner," badly.*]

DUNCAN. "Delegation from the Consolidated Railways Corporation, in reference to mobilization."

GORDON. Tell them next week.

DUNCAN. "Delegation from the Women's International Peace Fellowship."

GORDON. [*Looks up, listens.*] What's that noise, Duncan?

DUNCAN. The national anthem, Mr. President. That's their demonstration.

GORDON. Do they want to see me now?

DUNCAN. I can hold them off until tomorrow.

GORDON. Can you stand that another day?

DUNCAN. If *you* can, sir.

GORDON. Let them demonstrate. They've been bullied long enough.

[MRS. GORDON *enters.*]

MRS. GORDON. Good morning, Mr. Duncan. John, dear, you must have some breakfast.

GORDON. I've just had another pot of coffee.

MRS. GORDON. But you were up all night. I'll have a tray sent up to you.

GORDON. No, dear, please. I'll eat something later.

MRS. GORDON. You're quite sure you're all right.

GORDON. Quite. How's Robert?

MRS. GORDON. He isn't up yet. Too much party. Are you sure there is nothing I could do to help?

GORDON. Yes—send me another pot of coffee in about an hour.

MRS. GORDON. See that he gets something to eat, Mr. Duncan. [*She exits.*]

GORDON. Has the Congressional committee arrived?

DUNCAN. Mr. Fitzgerald, sir. The others are expected immediately.

GORDON. I'm expecting Fulton first. [*Takes up a sheaf from a pile of notes and clippings.*] What are these?

DUNCAN. Last night's clippings, Mr. President. But that was before Manila was taken. You can hardly be interested now.

GORDON. [*Taking up the papers, and running them*

over.] Yes, yes! [*Reads.*] War meetings in New York, Boston, Baltimore, another in Chicago.—The country on fire! If all this happened before Manila, in God's name what's happening now?

DUNCAN. [*Handing* GORDON *newspapers.*] The morning papers, sir. A mob attacked the Japanese Consulate at San Francisco. The Consul was saved by the police and the National Guard.

GORDON. Turn about! A consul for an ambassador! That's the way it goes. [*Looks at another pile.*] What are these letters clipped together?

DUNCAN. The anti-war communications and resolutions.

GORDON. Who's represented in it?

DUNCAN. Some peace societies, a number of conscientious objectors, and a few members of your Congress.

GORDON. Not very weighty. So that's my support.

DUNCAN. Have you finished your coffee?

GORDON. [*Finishing his coffee.*] Yes, thank you. You never speak personally, Duncan. Before we start the grind, I'd like to hear you say what *you* think of it?

DUNCAN. [*Tries to smile.*] I think, sir, as long as war is regarded as wicked, it will always have its fascinations. When it is looked upon as vulgar, it will cease to be popular.

GORDON. Is that your own philosophy?

DUNCAN. [*Taking tray from desk.*] No, sir. It was Oscar Wilde's. [*Starts for door.*]

[*Enter* MISS FOLWELL *with a report.*]

FOLWELL. I'll take that tray. Mr. Henley was just here with a note for the President.

DUNCAN. What did you do with him?

FOLWELL. Sent him away and took his note.

GORDON. Good for you.—Let me have it, please.

DUNCAN. I'll take the tray. [*Exit* DUNCAN, *with tray.*]

GORDON. Anything new in this?

FOLWELL. The note pasted on the front. Henley wants to amend his figures on Koyé's followers in Japanese provinces. His estimates in his reports were much too low.

GORDON. [*Looks at it quickly.*] Can his figures be correct?

FOLWELL. They're the latest, and I am sure they are correct.

GORDON. [*His attention riveted on the paper.*] That Jap's a wonder. If he only doesn't lose his head. . . .

FOLWELL. Yes, sir. He's in danger of it.

GORDON. So am I.—Has the Japanese Ambassador replied to my invitation?

FOLWELL. Not yet, Mr. President. We've had no word from the Embassy.

[*Enter* DUNCAN.]

GORDON. What is it, Duncan?

DUNCAN. The Secretary of State is here, sir.

GORDON. Show him in, Duncan.

DUNCAN. Yes, sir. [*Exit* DUNCAN.]

FOLWELL. I have copies of the Foreign Relations documents you asked for in my desk—if you should need them——

GORDON. Oh, for the committee. Just keep your eye on me, as usual.

FOLWELL. Thank you, Mr. President. I will. [*Takes some of the letters from* GORDON *and goes to door.*]

[*Enter* DUNCAN *with* SECRETARY DICKINSON.]

DUNCAN. The Secretary of State.

GORDON. Good morning, Mr. Dickinson.

DICKINSON. Good morning, Mr. President. Good morning, Miss Folwell.

FOLWELL. Good morning, Mr. Dickinson.

GORDON. No interruptions, Duncan, until Mr. Fulton turns up.

DUNCAN. Yes, sir. [*Exit* MISS FOLWELL *and* DUNCAN.]

GORDON. I wanted to see you, Dickinson. Please sit down. I'm glad you've come.

DICKINSON. [*Sits down, deliberately.*] Mr. President, I have this order—[*Takes it from pocket, with others.*]—directing me to send protests and regrets to the Japanese Government, and to request withdrawal of the Japanese forces from Manila.

GORDON. Yes, Dickinson.—"In the interest of peace and good-will."

DICKINSON. In the interest of peace and good-will. [*Puts note on desk.*] The message has been sent exactly as directed. Here is a copy. [GORDON *takes but does not read it.*] Also, Mr. President, I have this memorandum of your orders to the Secretary of War and to the Secretary of the Navy.

GORDON. Yes.—The orders have been issued by those departments. [*A pause.* GORDON *is anxious to know the next move. He puts down copy of order.*] I was up all night reading dispatches, editorials, pro and con—feeling for something to give me strength. I think I was really waiting for your vote of confidence.

DICKINSON. *Why* didn't you consult me, Gordon?

GORDON. My hand was forced.

DICKINSON. You won't be able to hold your Cabinet together.

GORDON. Are there others, besides Aldrich?

DICKINSON. There will be.—Congress will undoubtedly declare war against the Japanese Government. In the clash between you and Congress, one will go to pieces.

GORDON. We shall see.

DICKINSON. Japan won't be idle, while we wait. She's taken Manila. Hawaii may follow—San Francisco's next.

GORDON. She has your protest, and she'll be . . . confused.—She wouldn't dare.

DICKINSON. Confused at what? Our expression of regret?

GORDON. At our inaction!—If we don't move, neither can Japan. That's true in *any* contest. Time out!—Meanwhile, we'll find some way to arbitrate.

DICKINSON. [*With a gesture of impatience.*] You know our last chance to arbitrate with Japan went up in smoke when Yato was appointed Premier!

GORDON. I'm not bothered by Yato. I've faced him before, at League of Nations conferences.

DICKINSON. Gordon, I've been in the Government, one way or another, since Taft went to The Hague. He thought that would settle everything; so did I. But in a few years we discovered that jurists can't prevent wars, nor League delegates either. All they can do is fight over the remains, and the people are interested in another kind of fight.

GORDON. I'm counting on the people.

DICKINSON. They're mad.

GORDON. Because they've been bitten by mad dogs. Well, I've got a cure for that.

DICKINSON. What cure?

GORDON. I'll give them just as good a chance to get excited about peace as Brainard has given them to get excited about war.

DICKINSON. People care precious little about peace in a situation like this.

GORDON. Did you ever stop to think, Dickinson, why people always choose war in a crisis? Because they're never given the opportunity to choose anything else. The moment trouble begins, press, politicians, pulpits start baying for war. [*With great earnestness.*] But what if peace has a decent chance? What if people were asked *not* to fight, as urgently as they are now asked to fight?

DICKINSON. All very fine. But that's Utopia, and Utopia is a thousand years off. The time for *appeal* has gone by. It's now a matter of *action.*

GORDON. I've already acted.

DICKINSON. A few more quixotic gestures like the one you made last night, and the Government will be taken out of your hands——

GORDON. My fate's not important. I'm thinking of the nation, the world.

DICKINSON [*decisively*]. And their fate, too! Why, Gordon, today—tomorrow——

GORDON. [*With dignity and strength.*] I'm not concerned with today, or tomorrow—or the day after tomorrow—or the day after that. I'm thinking of ten years, a hundred years. . . . [*Stops, then, after a pause, turns appealingly to* DICKINSON.] Can't you see what it will mean to men in the future for a country like ours to come up against a great and terrible and righteous provocation to fight—and *refuse!*

DICKINSON. There's no precedent.

GORDON. That's the trouble. All the glorious examples are on the side of war. Well, we've got to break that chain!

DICKINSON. We can't.

GORDON. We can try! [*Rises.*] One precedent on the side of peace may be enough. At any rate, it will be a beginning. One nation challenged to fight, *forced* to fight—and refusing to fight! [*Pause.*] That might open doors . . . and reveal kingdoms. . . . [*Another pause.*] If there's a chance—any kind of a chance—what does it matter what happens to me, or to my administration?

DICKINSON. It matters to me! As a member of your Cabinet, I'd like to know how you'll get along without Aldrich—even Fulton . . .

GORDON. Fulton won't leave us—not *now.*—We'll have a Cabinet.

DICKINSON. [*Rises.*] You're a brave man, Gordon. Also, if I may say so, a very foolish one.

GORDON. Perhaps the world needs fools. I can't see that the wise men have got us so very far. Let me ask you one question before you go. [DICKINSON *turns.*] What would *you* do, if you were in my place?

DICKINSON. [*Pause.*] I don't know.

GORDON. Would you do what Brainard has done?

DICKINSON. No—a thousand times no!

GORDON. Then what alternative is there, to Brainard or myself? Haven't we either got to make war—and make it now, with all the strength, all the savagery, there is in us? Or haven't we got to make peace, and make it now—with all the strength, all the sanctity, there is in us? [*Pause.*] What would you do, if you were in my place?

DICKINSON. [*Broken.*] I don't know. *I don't know!*

GORDON. Well, I *do* know! [*Stops, as though caught up and inspired.*] I'm going to prove that it's possible to keep peace when war seems inevitable. I may succeed— [*Pause.*] and—if—I—*fail* . . . well, failure can't be any worse than war! [*Short silence.*]

DICKINSON. Gordon, I'm no wise man—and I'm no fool, either. I don't believe in your ideas, not for a damn. But I believe in *you.* You've got courage—and, God help me, I'll see you through. [*They shake hands.*]

GORDON [*very simply*]. Thank you, Dickinson! I may be the blind leading the blind. But I feel something, somebody, has me by the hand, and is pulling me along. I feel . . . I think I see. . . . [*Pause, and then, like a dedication.*] . . . I'm going to follow to the end! [*Knock.*] Oh! Mr. Fulton! [*Enter* DUNCAN.] Show Mr. Fulton in. . . . Until later, Dickinson.

DICKINSON. Yes, Mr. President. [*Exit* DICKINSON.]

DUNCAN. He's on the 'phone, sir.

GORDON. On the 'phone? [*He pauses, then takes up receiver.*] Hello? . . . Yes, Fulton. . . . I was expecting you to come in. Any luck with Aldrich? [*Pause.*] I see. . . . No, of course. Thank you. . . . You did your best. We'll have to get along without him. I'll need you all the more. . . . We can talk when you come over to . . . What's that? [*Pause.*] Oh. . . . If you feel that way, naturally. . . . I'm sorry. . . . I don't know what else to say. . . . No, friendship can't count now, of course. . . . If you must, you must. I had hoped. . . . Very well. Good-bye, Fulton. [*Slowly he hangs up the receiver, looks at* DUNCAN.] Well, Duncan! Tonight you and

I may be the only members of the Government left.

DUNCAN. Has Mr. Fulton resigned? [GORDON *nods.*] I thought he was waiting to hear how you made out with the Congressional committee!

GORDON. Apparently he couldn't wait. [DUNCAN *goes to his desk and angrily throws down some papers.*] Thanks, Duncan. That's just the way *I* feel. Is the committee waiting?

DUNCAN. Not all of them, but Admiral James is outside and spoiling for a fight.

GORDON. Let's have him in!

[DUNCAN *exits.* GORDON *shows a moment of anxiety, then steels himself. Enter* DUNCAN *and* ADMIRAL JAMES, *who is a vigorous, quick-spoken type, in dress uniform.*]

DUNCAN. Admiral James, sir. [*Exits.*]

GORDON. How do you do, Admiral James. How are you?

JAMES. Good morning, Mr. President.

GORDON. Sit down.

JAMES. Thank you.

GORDON. Have a cigar.

JAMES. Thank you. I came to see you about the orders to the Navy Department——

GORDON. Have a light.

JAMES. —and to Admiral Graham, issued last night.

GORDON. Well——

JAMES. What I have to say can be said quickly.—These orders, sir, are impossible.

GORDON. Impossible?

JAMES. Pardon the word, Mr. President. But—forgive me—you do not *know* what the orders mean.

GORDON [*very politely*]. Perhaps you can enlighten me.

JAMES. That the campaign for the war with Japan is disrupted—the whole machinery of the attack broken to pieces!

GORDON. Machinery of attack on Japan? I don't understand.

JAMES. No, Mr. President, you don't know these plans. It was my first duty to inform you—but I didn't dream that last night, on your first day in office . . .

GORDON. It is not too late now. Please tell me what you came here to say.

JAMES. It may be too late! [*More confidentially.*] Mr. President, the trouble with Japan has been brewing for months. It was evident some time ago that war was at least possible. Under these conditions, of course, it becomes necessary for *us* to prepare . . .

GORDON. Us? To whom do you refer?

JAMES. The Government—the Navy Department. We have plans in our files for the Japanese war worked out in every detail. The moment war is in the wind, we have to move, to get ready. The *first blow,* Mr. President, is all-important. It was the day that Mr. Brainard sent his ultimatum that he ordered the General Staff . . .

GORDON [*interrupting*]. He *knew* that meant war!

JAMES. . . . to set their plans in motion.

GORDON. You mean, to start the campaign.

JAMES. To get ready. The President took personal charge. . . .

GORDON. Of course!

JAMES. [*Rises.*] Everything was done in this room. Look here. . . . [ALMIRAL JAMES *goes to left wall and pulls down a large map of the Pacific area. The map is marked with heavy clusters of short red lines, indicating the places shown by the* ADMIRAL.] This is how the fleet is actually stationed at this moment. Graham's ships are unimportant. The country thinks, you probably thought, that they constitute the main fleet, held in harbor all this time. But the fleet sailed days ago under sealed orders. Graham's ships are only a rear guard. . . .

GORDON [*aghast*]. A smoke-screen for the people —and for me!

JAMES. Look at these little red lines. . . . [*Pointing to the map.*] Here, a hundred miles off

Guam, is Taylor's squadron. Brook's battleships are here, two hundred miles northeast of the Philippines.—The submarines are here, under the lee of Formosa. The cruisers, our fastest ships, are stationed here under Morrison, not far from Hawaii. Fifty squadrons of Navy planes are ready at Honolulu. Quick orders will mobilize the fleet like the closing of a fan. Japan won't have a *chance*. . . .

GORDON. Exactly!—Now I am beginning to understand.

JAMES. Yes, sir. I knew you would.— [*Moves closer to map.*] You see, Mr. President . . .

GORDON. I know now why Japan took Manila.

JAMES. Manila?——

GORDON. [*Studies the map, then turns abruptly.*] Do you suppose Japan was ignorant of what you were doing? The Japanese Admiralty undoubtedly has this same map hanging on the walls of its offices. And not intending to be caught napping, *they* struck the first blow you talk about!

JAMES. You mean they *knew* of our plans?

GORDON. Their desperate action proves it! You're a bad officer, James. How long, for instance, do you expect that submarine squadron to last, in that position?—But you're a worse statesman, giving Japan an excuse to attack, and a reason for making war. Brainard's work!—But never mind! We'll stop all this. It's not too late.—Those ships are coming home.

JAMES [*speechless*]. But—but Mr. President, that's why I've come here, to protest . . .

GORDON. Those ships, Admiral, are coming *home*. Every battleship, cruiser, submarine—if they are not already destroyed. I won't have one of those ships at sea—not a prow nor a gun pointed at Japan. You will return to your Department, Admiral, at once, and confirm the orders I issued last night.—I sent direct to Graham. Now you send to Taylor and Brooks and Morrison, and any other commander or station. Ships to turn east, to the home base—at full speed.

JAMES. [*Pause.*] But Mr. President—this will be fatal . . .

GORDON. Fatal to what—to whom?

JAMES. To all the plans for this war.

GORDON. What war? Explain yourself.

JAMES. Mr. President, if you please—I have no time for this. You know that war with Tokio is imminent. Our plans have been made. . . .

GORDON. Why?

JAMES. Because we must be prepared. Plans have to be set in motion.

GORDON. Why!

JAMES. This war has *started* . . .

GORDON. So I see!—So this is your *news*.

JAMES. . . . and you are countermanding orders, upsetting naval plans, spreading confusion. Don't you realize, if you will pardon me, that these plans are like a machine, cog fitting into cog—and that if there's a slip anywhere, the whole thing goes to smash? Mr. President, we have started the machine, and it must go on!

GORDON. So that's what armies and navies are—a machine! That's why wars get started and then can't be stopped. And I'm just a cog in your set-up, and Brainard's!—Well, it's been that way often enough in the past, I guess. But it won't be so again—not here! I'm no part of a machine, Admiral James. I'm still a man, and in this office, a free agent. If the Government, and your Navy, is a machine, then my hand is on the clutch. I can throw it into reverse as easily as straight ahead.—Admiral, you have heard my orders . . . !

JAMES. [*In despair, growing angry.*] This is impossible! It will upset everything!

GORDON. I intend it to upset everything.

JAMES. We shall lose the war.—Our plans—we can never carry them out! Look at this map. . . .

GORDON. [*In a fierce outburst of anger.*] Roll up that map! I have no further use for it—neither have you.—It's ancient history, as dead as Cæsar's maps of Gaul! [ADMIRAL JAMES *hesi-*

tates. GORDON *rushes to the wall in a fury, seizes the map with both hands and sweeps it to the floor. A silence.* GORDON *looks at the empty space on the wall.*] That's a good place for a new map, clean, unmarked.—There'll be no wars on it! [*Turns to* JAMES.] Forgive me, Admiral. Please don't think that I'm blaming you alone. I know that you were acting under Brainard's orders.—But now, you will remember, if you please, that you are acting under mine.

JAMES. [*Bewildered.*] I understand, sir.

GORDON. [*Pressing button on desk.*] You will be so good as to return to your Department and act immediately.

JAMES. Yes, Mr. President. [*Walks to the door, and stops.*] Will these orders apply to the naval aviation plans as well?

GORDON. Naturally. [*Enter* DUNCAN.] Admiral James is leaving, Duncan.—Are the members of the committee waiting?

DUNCAN. Yes, Mr. President. [DUNCAN *starts to go.*]

GORDON. One moment, Duncan.—Good morning, Admiral James.

JAMES. Good morning, Mr. President. [*Exit* JAMES.]

GORDON. [*After a pause, to himself; walks up and down.*] Blundering schoolboy tactics! What's happened to their *minds*—if they had any! [*To* DUNCAN, *who has picked up the map.*] Don't take that away. Roll it up, I may need it. A machine! *I'll* show them who runs their machine . . . ! [GORDON *suddenly, with quick decision, sits at his desk and writes a brief note.*] Duncan . . .

DUNCAN. Yes, sir.

GORDON. Have this note delivered at once. You can send it by a Secret Service messenger.

DUNCAN. Yes, Mr. President.

[MISS FOLWELL *enters.*]

FOLWELL. Mr. President.

GORDON. Yes, Miss Folwell.

FOLWELL. I'm sorry, but Mr. Turner is here with bad news.

GORDON. Well?

FOLWELL. It's all over with Koyé. He's lost his head!

GORDON. Killed?

FOLWELL. No, not yet. [*Referring to papers in her hand.*] But he led a peace demonstration in Tokio last night. He was arrested and put in jail.

GORDON. Arrested? Is Mr. Turner outside?

FOLWELL. Yes, Mr. President.

GORDON. Bring him in.

FOLWELL. Yes, Mr. President. [*Exits.*]

GORDON. Another blow, Duncan. [TURNER *and* MISS FOLWELL *enter.*] You have press dispatches, Turner?

TURNER. Yes, Mr. President. A U.P. announcing Koyé's arrest. An A.P. stating that a dozen other leaders have been arrested.

GORDON. Any other details?

TURNER. Yes, I called the *Times* office. They have a long dispatch from their Tokio correspondent. He states that General Nogatu, Minister of War, is in control, and is breaking up the peace movement.

DUNCAN. A peace movement can't be broken up by the military. They can only drive it underground.

FOLWELL. That doesn't help us now.

GORDON. You're right, Miss Folwell. [*Picking up Henley's report from his desk.*] A million followers, and no leader!

TURNER. Sorry to bring you bad news, sir.

GORDON. That's all right, Turner.

TURNER. Yes, sir. [*Exits.*]

FOLWELL. Oh, Mr. Duncan, the committee is waiting.

DUNCAN. Thank you. [MISS FOLWELL *exits.*]

GORDON. [*Handing over the note he had been writing.*] Send that at once, Duncan.

DUNCAN. [*Looks at note, then at* GORDON, *surprised.*] If it is possible. I'll try his hotel, sir.

GORDON. If he's left there, try the trains. He must not leave Washington. *Now* inform the committee that I'm ready to take them on!

DUNCAN. Yes, sir. [*Exits with note.*]

[*Enter the committee.* SENATOR BRIGHT *with* SENATOR HILL *and* REPRESENTATIVES WILMOT, FITZGERALD, *and* SMITH. TURNER *follows them in. All talking.*]

BRIGHT. Good morning, Mr. President. . . .

GORDON. Good morning, Mr. Bright.—Gentlemen, will you make yourselves comfortable, please?

[*He remains at desk.* BRIGHT *and* HILL *near* GORDON, *on chairs.* SMITH *goes to sofa.* TURNER *arranges chairs for other two.*

TURNER. [*To* WILMOT, *cheerily.*] Good work, Mr. Wilmot. That was a nice jump Jennings Steel took this morning—90 to 110. Broke the amateur record, the boys tell me.

WILMOT. I'm here to consult the President—not to quote steel prices. Mr. President.

GORDON. Mr. Wilmot.—

WILMOT. [*Goes to* BRIGHT.] What's the press doing in on this conference, Mr. Bright?

BRIGHT. I didn't know it was in.—Have you any objections?

WILMOT. I thought this was a special committee. Do you need the press?

HILL. What about it, Mr. President?

GORDON. I certainly have no objections to being reported. Have any of you?

FITZGERALD. None whatever! I *like* to be heard. [*All laugh.*]

WILMOT. We'll all be heard soon enough. Mr. Bright, as chairman, I ask you to exclude the press. This is Government business.

BRIGHT. If it's agreeable to the President.

GORDON. Certainly, certainly. I mistook the people for the Government, momentarily.—Turner, will you send Miss Folwell in, to take notes? [*Exit* TURNER, *with a rude gesture to* WILMOT. *They settle themselves.*] Let's get down to business, gentlemen. You have asked to see me about the state of war now threatening the country.

BRIGHT. Yes, Mr. President. The events of the last forty-eight hours make immediate and drastic action necessary. We thought we could hasten matters by finding out your intentions in this crisis.

GORDON. That can't be in doubt, Mr. Bright, after what I said yesterday.

FITZGERALD. And after your explicit orders last night.

GORDON. I propose to do everything in my power to find terms of reconciliation with Japan. I shall ask for the full support not only of my party, but of Congress as a whole, in my policy of peace.

FITZGERALD. [*Rises.*] Peace!—After Manila? Do you expect the people of this nation . . . !
[*Enter* MISS FOLWELL.]

HILL. Please, Fitzgerald. We won't get anywhere with that attitude.

BRIGHT. I'd like to ask Mr. Fitzgerald to let *me* speak, as chairman of his committee.

FITZGERALD. Go ahead, go ahead. Overruled.
[*He sits down, apart, in his chair.*]

BRIGHT [*pompously*]. We have organized this committee, Mr. President, with the consent of our fellow members of Congress, to represent the sentiments of that body as a whole. We seem to be of a single mind. We are for war—at the earliest moment it can be declared and begun. After what Japan has done, there is no other course open. We expect a declaration of war within twenty-four hours.

WILMOT [*officiously*]. You must have foreseen that, Mr. President. Or did you think, by ordering the fleet to return to San Francisco, that Congress would be brow-beaten into forgetting its duty?

FITZGERALD. And the people frightened into betraying the glorious tradition of their heritage!

GORDON. The American people is a peace-loving people.

WILMOT. Yes. But not a cowardly people!

FITZGERALD. [*Rises. With platform fervor.*] Mr.

President, may I remind you that you are sitting in the chair of Washington, of Lincoln? Two great Presidents, who led the people, like Moses in the wilderness, through the Red Sea of war! . . . [*Sits.*]

GORDON [*patiently*]. Quite, Mr. Fitzgerald.—I realize that I occupy the chair of the great Presidents of the Republic. The demands of that office, laid down by . . .

HILL [*drily*]. I believe the committee knows the elements of government.

FITZGERALD [*continuing*]. In all our *glorious* history . . . !

BRIGHT [*interrupting*]. If we could get on with the proceedings, Mr. Representative.

GORDON. Excuse me for interrupting this historical recitation. We are not living in the age of Washington or Lincoln. We are not bound by their acts.

FITZGERALD. So! We must repudiate the fathers of the nation!

GORDON. I repudiate nobody. I remind you of certain facts. Washington was a gentleman slaveholder, as well as a general. Are we still to hold slaves? Lincoln called the Civil War, which he tried to prevent, the "judgment of the Almighty" upon our sins.—I admit that America had a glorious war record when war was considered glorious. But it is no longer glorious—nor even excusable!

[MISS FOLWELL, *still holding her notes, rises and places a document at the* PRESIDENT'S *hand and resumes her seat.*]

HILL [*drily*]. I am a Californian, Mr. President, and ignorant. Will telling Japan that war is inexcusable prevent her from invading our territory?

GORDON. Will declaring war! [*He takes up the document from his desk.*] It was not many years ago that Congress authorized an Ambassador from the United States to sign this document, the Kellogg Pact, which makes war a crime, and abandons it as an instrument of national policy! To me this treaty is as sacred a document as the Declaration of Independence or the Constitution.

FITZGERALD. [*Rises.*] I challenge you, Mr. President, to stand by the grave of the Unknown Soldier and announce that to the nation!

BRIGHT. We're here to try to understand the President's viewpoint, Fitzgerald. We're familiar with yours.

SMITH. I quite agree, Mr. Bright. Thank you!

GORDON. I regret the absence of the press.—But we are faced with a practical question: I have issued orders to stop the war. You say you will declare war. . . . Do we divide in the face of the enemy?

FITZGERALD. Divide rather than retreat!

GORDON. I advocate no retreat. But I insist on a new line of attack!

FITZGERALD. Attack! Do you call it attack to lay down your arms, send ships scuttling home, offer diplomatic apologies. . . . Attack!

SMITH. [*Rises. Steps to back of chair.*] Mr. Bright, if I may be excused from Mr. Fitzgerald's committee . . .

FITZGERALD. I'm here to state what I think!

SMITH. Pardon me. I thought you had, Mr. Fitzgerald.

GORDON. I understand the difficult position you are in, Mr. Smith. I'm in one myself. Please stay.

SMITH. If you wish, Mr. President.

WILMOT. Are you going back on your word, Mr. Smith?

SMITH. [*Growing angry.*] My word to whom? I promised in the campaign to support the President. That's what I want to do, but——

GORDON. I need your support, Mr. Smith. I take it you are not in accord with this committee.

SMITH. Not with their methods, Mr. President. [*Looks at* BRIGHT.] I don't believe in bullying.

BRIGHT. We are not attempting to force the President's hand . . .

SMITH. Aren't you, indeed, Mr. Bright? It seems to me that the vote represented by this committee in Congress is being used for just that reason.

WILMOT [*gruffly*]. You're quite right, Smith. And the votes you carry will not affect the decision very much one way or another. That's plain speaking, but you asked for it.

SMITH. How do you know? Gibbs and Elliott are with me.

HILL. That's where you're wrong, Mr. Smith. Gibbs has decided in favor of the declaration. I just saw him. You are alone.

SMITH. They both promised me that if I could make myself heard . . . !

FITZGERALD. You can't be. They've both been persuaded to vote with us.

SMITH. Persuaded! What did you offer them? Steel dividends?

GORDON. Now, now. Let's not count votes so soon, Mr. Smith, are *you* with me?

SMITH. [*Pause.—He looks around at the others.*] I wish I could say yes, Mr. President.

GORDON. Can't you?

SMITH. I wanted to. That was my purpose in serving on this committee. But the more I hear of its tactics, the more convinced I am—that it's no use.

GORDON. But will you personally vote for the declaration?

SMITH. I've waited, like many others, to see what you could do, sir, to prevent war. Now I know that you have no chance.—I cannot sacrifice my position for nothing.—I'm afraid I must cast my vote with this committee, for war. [*He looks at* GORDON *hopelessly.*]

GORDON. I'm sorry, Mr. Smith.——

WILMOT. Mr. Smith, like the rest of us, realizes that we represent a hundred and fifty million people. . . .

GORDON. Are you sure, Mr. Wilmot? It seems to me that *I* represent the people even better than —you. The duties of my office are as sacred to me as yours. They weigh very heavily on me. And I will *not* betray the confidence of the men and women who put me in office by refusing to hear my conscience. I insist on my right to lay down a policy for this nation, and to demand your support—until it has been proven ineffectual.

WILMOT. Your policy has already been proven ineffectual, and dangerous! The Japanese fleet has taken Manila!

GORDON. That action was in answer to Brainard's policy before I ever announced *mine.*

FITZGERALD. [*Rises.*] That's quibbling. The

Japanese knew a pacifist was going into the White House. They took advantage of our weakness. Within twenty-four hours we've found out what your reputation can do for us!

WILMOT. [*Rises.*] You reminded us a moment ago of the duties of your office, Mr. President. Well, now let me remind you of the duties of *our* office. Under the Constitution, Congress alone has power to declare war. The leadership you talk about has shifted in the night to the other end of the Avenue. We are here to state in the name of the people that Congress will declare war against Japan the moment the resolution can be passed. We expect you to act accordingly.

BRIGHT. Nothing else is possible, Mr. President. Your orders *must* be withdrawn.

GORDON. Gentlemen, are you definitely agreed with this decision? Mr. Hill?

HILL. We are in unanimous agreement. The naval operations and the mobilization must go on.

FITZGERALD. They should never have been stopped.

WILMOT. Insane! Stopping activities when anyone in the country could see we'd have to have war! *You* must have seen it.

GORDON. I acted with clear mind and deliberate purpose. I did not hesitate to weigh possibilities.

BRIGHT. You must have considered we would vote for war.

GORDON. I considered it not only possible but entirely probable.

FITZGERALD [*to others*]. There you have his own admission of guilt.

GORDON. What am I guilty of? If you're talking of my legal rights—what about your own, gentlemen. This declaration of war that you are proposing to pass . . .

WILMOT. What about it?

GORDON. I question its legality. I doubt if you can move. It's time we found out whether you or I have the power in this crisis. Miss Folwell, ask Secretary Dickinson to come in, please.

FOLWELL. Yes, Mr. President. [*Exit* MISS FOLWELL.]

WILMOT. What's the Secretary of State got to do with this situation?

FITZGERALD. Mr. Bright, what are we up against now?—I move we adjourn.

BRIGHT. Mr. President, the committee would like to know why it must consult with your Secretary of State at this time.

GORDON. Mr. Dickinson is a jurist—the former Chief Justice of the Supreme Court—an authority on constitutional law. I want his advice.

WILMOT. On what point, Mr. President?

GORDON. There are questions to be settled here before you can declare war.

WILMOT. What do you mean, Mr. President?

SMITH. Wait for the Secretary of State. We're not going to be tricked out of any rights that belong to us as Representatives.

HILL. The enemy headed for our coasts, and we bicker about jurists and constitutional law. [*In angry disgust.*] I'm through! [*Starts for the door.*]

BRIGHT. Wait a moment, Mr. Hill. Let's not get excited.

WILMOT. Have you anything to say, Smith?

SMITH. What can I say?

BRIGHT. Now then, Mr. President, we would like to know just what move you intend to make on which you ask advice.

GORDON. Quite simple! You have told me that you propose tomorrow to declare war. But you have no right to do so without formal request from the Chief Executive.

BRIGHT. That's a formality which you could not possibly withhold, Mr. President.

FITZGERALD. Congress declares war.

GORDON. Only on recommendation of the President! In the absence of a message formally asking Congress for a declaration of war, which I shall not send. . . .

HILL. We shall proceed without you.

[*A wild confusion of speeches flung at the* PRESIDENT *all at once.*]

BRIGHT. We are declaring war in the interests of the people we represent.

SMITH. Wait till we find out if we can. What's the sense in brawling?

HILL. At a time like this to have to listen to a lot of copy-book talk!

FITZGERALD. We're here in Washington to protect the safety of our homes, our wives, our children,——

WILMOT. I should say so, and *so damned quick* you'll be left——

GORDON. [*Breaking into the confusion.*] Just a minute, gentlemen. You seem to forget what you have all reminded me of—that *I* am now President.

WILMOT. Yes, Mr. President—but I happen to know the powers of the Chief Executive.

FITZGERALD. You are exceeding your authority, sir.

GORDON. Am I, Mr. Fitzgerald?

[*Enter* MISS FOLWELL.]

FOLWELL. The Secretary of State.

[*Enter* DICKINSON.]

GORDON. Let's see if I am! Mr. Secretary, we have reached a crisis in this meeting. I have made a statement . . .

FITZGERALD. A defiance!

GORDON. . . . a statement to the effect that I shall refuse, as President, to ask the Congress for a declaration of war against Japan.

BRIGHT. A state of war which already exists, Mr. Secretary.

GORDON. I shall send in no official recommendation upon which Congress can act. In that case, I am insisting Congress has no legal right to act.

HILL. This is nonsense, Mr. Secretary.

WILMOT. We object to this wanton interference with the powers of Congress.

GORDON. The powers of the Executive! . . . Mr. Secretary, what is your opinion?

DICKINSON [*with deliberation*]. No, Mr. President. I am very sorry, but in this case, if I understand the situation, the Executive *has* no power. As a matter of history, you are quite right. Congress has never declared war except at the express request of the Executive. But this is custom, and not law. The right to declare war is an absolute right vested by the Constitution in Congress alone. On this issue, Mr. President, I cannot sustain you. In my judgment the Supreme Court would not do so. Congress is now in session. And has the power to declare war. You cannot prevent it.

[*The tension breaks.* GORDON *is immediately*

alone, as the MEN *surround* DICKINSON—*ad lib.*]

BRIGHT [*cheerfully*]. Thank you, Mr. Secretary. You have greatly relieved the situation.

DICKINSON. But not ended it, I trust. You have the power to declare war. But I have spoken with the President, this morning. He intends to preserve the peace—and if it is in any way possible, so do I.

WILMOT. You know it's *not* possible, Mr. Secretary.

DICKINSON. I understand the Constitution, Mr. Wilmot. I also know its spirit: "In Union There Is Strength."—Good morning. [*He starts to go.*]

GORDON. Don't go, Mr. Dickinson.

BRIGHT. Mr. President, we will leave you, with your permission. The Secretary of State has said what the Constitution answers to your threat.

HILL. You have our decision. There is no further reason for our staying.

GORDON [*sharply*]. Yes, Senator Hill, there is. [*The men stop, arrested by his tone.*] My answer to all this is brief. You will have time to hear it. You gentlemen have said you will declare war. Mr. Dickinson has said that I cannot prevent that declaration. But there's one thing I can do. I can refuse to recognize or act upon your declaration of war when it is passed.

HILL. You mean you will *veto* the resolution?

GORDON. No, Mr. Hill. That's technically within my power. Under the circumstances, knowing the temper of your committee and Congress, it would be a useless gesture.

HILL. You're right. We'd pass it anyway. I'm glad we agree. If there's no more point in debate—I'm going.

GORDON. If you will allow me, gentlemen! You have stated often enough the duties I owe my office. Perhaps now you'll believe me when I say I *know* these duties. With my position as Commander-in-Chief of the Army and Navy, gentlemen, you have no right to interfere. I know I'm right about that, Mr. Dickinson.

DICKINSON. Without any doubt.

HILL. We don't want to interfere.

GORDON. The military is my province; its plans, its movements belong exclusively to me. You may declare war, but I conduct it. And it is my intention to conduct this war of yours in my own way. If it is to be war—and *you* must decide that, Mr. Bright—and Mr. Hill, and Mr. Wilmot, and the rest of you—let me tell you flatly that it will be war without military operations, without fighting. Armies and navies will have no part in *this* war . . .

BRIGHT. War without armies is impossible!

FITZGERALD. The man is out of his mind!

GORDON. Out of my mind, Mr. Fitzgerald? Well, if you think I am, you will be wise not to pass your declaration. The moment you do, you clothe me with dictatorial authority. As Commander-in-Chief of the Army and Navy in time of war, I rule with an absolute control never existing in time of peace!

WILMOT. He's trying to threaten us!—He can't do that . . . !

GORDON. I *am* threatening you, Mr. Wilmot, as you've tried to threaten me!—Go ahead with your war resolution. Give me the power, if you insist. I do not ask it. I do not want it. I have no desire to command armies and navies. But let me tell you this, gentlemen. If you give me this power, I shall use it in my own way.

BRIGHT. Mr. President, you would not *dare* withhold the army and navy in case of war.

GORDON. That is exactly what I shall do. Pass your declaration. Put it through by unanimous vote of both Houses. Give it to the people! I promise you, that not a soldier in this land will march. Not one of our ships will sail. As Commander-in-Chief, these arms of the Government are in my control, and I tell you I will *not* use them for purposes of war! There's my answer to your threat. Make the most of it.

[*The men are non-plussed, then break into shouts of disapproval.*]

DICKINSON. [*Drawing* GORDON *aside.*] Gordon, listen to me. . . .

WILMOT. There you are, gentlemen! For three months I've been telling you the country'd elected a lunatic—and now he *proves* it!

[DUNCAN *enters.*]

SMITH. You called him a figurehead, Mr. Wilmot. You were wrong!

FITZGERALD. *Traitor,* you mean! This is *treason!*

BRIGHT. Mr. Fitzgerald! Not quite so fast!

FITZGERALD. There's our authority. Mr. Dickinson, I say this is treason. Am I right?

DICKINSON. I shouldn't go so far as to say that!

WILMOT. It is. He'll be ousted from office.

FITZGERALD. Bright, you're chairman. Tell the President we accuse him of *treason.*

GORDON. [*Who has been conferring with* DUNCAN *and* MISS FOLWELL.] *One minute,* please.—I hear a charge of treason. I'd like to answer your charge. I have a further witness to call.

WILMOT. We've had enough witnesses to know your position and ours, Mr. President!

GORDON. I think not. Duncan, show in the ex-President, Mr. Brainard. [*Pause.* DUNCAN *exits.*]

WILMOT. Mr. *Brainard!*

GORDON. Yes, Mr. Wilmot. You know my stand, but you don't know why I insist on taking it. Please wait, gentlemen. I haven't finished conferring with this committee from my Congress. —Gentlemen. [*Sits.*]

[*They sit down, slowly, wondering. Enter* DUNCAN, *followed by* BRAINARD, *a large forceful man. He is surprised to see the committee.*]

DUNCAN. Mr. Brainard.

GORDON. Come in, Mr. Brainard.

BRAINARD. Good morning, Mr. President.

GORDON. I'm glad we were able to reach you. You *know* these gentlemen, I presume.

BRAINARD. This is not exactly what I expected.

DICKINSON. How do you do, Mr. Brainard? [*They shake hands, somewhat to* BRAINARD'S *surprise. He goes to* WILMOT.]

BRAINARD. Well, Wilmot? What's this all about?

WILMOT. Don't ask me! Nobody knows.

BRAINARD. [*Turns to* FITZGERALD, HILL, *etc.*] You didn't expect me to be back so soon, did you? Well, to tell you the truth, neither did I. [*Laughs, attempting to cover his confusion.*] Hello, Senator! I thought I was out of this business!

HILL. We're all in it now, up to our necks.

GORDON. Miss Folwell, have you got all your notes ready?

MISS FOLWELL. Yes, Mr. President.—Shall I call Mr. Turner?

GORDON. You've guessed it. I want every paper and radio station in the country in on this.—Duncan, stand by.

[*Exit* MISS FOLWELL.]

BRAINARD. A committee in meeting—press secretaries, Mr. President? May I have some explanation?

GORDON. Immediately, Mr. Brainard. Sit down, please. [BRAINARD *sits.*] I asked you here expressly so that you might meet this committee in my presence.

BRAINARD. Why did you summon me?

[*Enter* MISS FOLWELL *with* TURNER.]

GORDON. First, let me introduce Mr. Turner.

BRAINARD [*coldly*]. I know Turner. I read his imaginary accounts of your action in the papers this morning.

TURNER. Thanks for the compliment, Mr. Brainard, but we don't have to make up stories any more. We get the facts from the White House.

BRAINARD. Do you mean those orders were actually issued?

GORDON. They were sent, and corroborated this morning.—Why?

BRAINARD. [*Amazed.*] Well!—If I must speak before these members of Congress——

GORDON. You speak before a wider audience. What *about* my orders, sir?

BRAINARD. I'm not questioning your authority. I'm merely afraid of what you may not *know*.

GORDON. What *you* have known all along, and what it was your duty to let me know, immediately.

BRAINARD [*to* BRIGHT]. Am I to stand trial before this committee?

BRIGHT. Mr. President, will you explain this proceeding?

GORDON. Certainly! Mr. Brainard has been in command of certain facts which were only given to me less than an hour ago, by Admiral James. —Yes, Mr. Brainard, he told me the entire plan —the disposition of the fleet—the military positions—everything.

BRAINARD. Then you realize what you have done.

GORDON. Perfectly.

BRAINARD. Thank God for that. I *knew* the newspaper accounts could not be complete.

GORDON. They were quite complete. I have not withdrawn my orders.

BRAINARD. Do you mean that . . . after you discovered the facts of the campaign . . .

GORDON. My orders stand. Admiral James is at the Navy Department offices now, sending instructions to every commander at sea to return to port tonight.

BRAINARD. [*Pause—simply.*] I don't believe you.

GORDON. Ask these gentlemen. Mr. Fulton has

also stopped your mobilization plans during the last twelve hours.

BRAINARD. Mr. Bright—has your committee heard this?

BRIGHT. We have heard everything, Mr. Brainard . . .

BRAINARD. Fitzgerald—Wilmot?

FITZGERALD. It's all true, so help me God. And more . . . !

WILMOT. The President informs us that in the event of Congress voting a war resolution, he will withdraw the army and navy and refuse to fight.

BRAINARD. Withdraw? On what authority?

GORDON. *You* should know. As Commander-in-Chief.

BRAINARD. But damn it, Gordon, we are at *war!*

DUNCAN [*intervening*]. "Mr. President," if you please.

BRAINARD. Japan has attacked us. She's captured Manila!

GORDON. Why?

BRAINARD. She's sunk our ships, and killed our men. . . .

GORDON. Why?

BRAINARD. She has, that's all. Refuse to fight her, now? That's malfeasance in office—it's betrayal of the people. . . .

GORDON. Go on! You must have more to say, Mr. Brainard!

BRAINARD. [*Rises.*] Yes, by God, I have. It's *treason!*

FITZGERALD. [*Jumps up.*] There! Treason, just as *I* said.

BRAINARD. Yes, and it should be dealt with as treason. Gentlemen, as a private citizen, I demand the impeachment of the President!

BRIGHT. [*Rises.*] Impeachment!——

GORDON. [*Rises.*] That's a very fine answer to my question, Mr. Brainard. And since you bring up the accusation, I shall turn it about—and tell the people of the country *where* the betrayal lies. [*To committee.*] You have heard Mr. Brainard's answer, gentlemen. He *has* no answer to explain the attack on our possessions. But there *is* an answer.

BRAINARD. You accuse me . . . !

GORDON. You'll let me speak now, sir. There is an accounting due this nation and this office. It's time you rendered it.

BRAINARD. Am I summoned here to answer your cross-examination? Am I on trial . . . ?

GORDON. Yes. That's exactly what you are. I demand an explanation. You say we are at war with Japan. I deny it.

BRAINARD. Indeed! Even a pacifist should recognize a state of war when he's in it!

GORDON. In any case, we were not at war yesterday, nor the day before.—It's true you sent an ultimatum three weeks ago that in its wording was practically an act of war. But by its terms you were bound to keep the peace until Japan replied. That period, by your own decree, was a truce, sacred to the work of reconciliation. You trusted Japan, for three weeks, to do the friendly thing —and what were you doing?

BRAINARD. What you're refusing to do now—protecting the nation!

GORDON. Two weeks ago, at the very moment you dispatched your ultimatum, you gave orders to the general staff of the navy to begin war with Japan!

BRAINARD. That's a lie!

DICKINSON. Brainard!——

GORDON. You sent a fleet to appointed positions in the Pacific, and left Graham behind with a skeleton squadron to blind our eyes. See here . . . ! [GORDON *takes up the map which has been lying on his desk and spreads it out.*] Look at this map! It hung there, gentlemen—for the plotting of President Brainard's war!

BRAINARD. One minute, Gordon!

GORDON. See these short red lines, in clusters? [*The committee draws near the desk.*] Admiral Taylor here at Guam, Brooks off the Philippines, Morrison west of Hawaii, here the submarines.

These ships were there today, until my orders were dispatched. They were stripped for action, their steam up night and day, their guns unlimbered, their crews under battle orders. Ready, you say? Yes, ready for the war that they themselves had made. See how they surrounded their prey—how they could close in at a moment's notice! [*Looks up.*] Gentlemen, this is making war when there is no war! And you are amazed that Japan has leaped into action and taken Manila! [*Leaves his desk and faces* BRAINARD.] If war comes to this country, Brainard—a long war, costing millions of lives and billions of dollars—you will be responsible. In time of peace, in hostility to a friendly nation, you made war. [*Pause.*] Well, Brainard, in time of war, if it is war, I shall make peace. If you had power as Commander-in-Chief to do the one, I as your successor have power to do the other. [*To the committee.*] Who will dispute me? In any case, that is what I am going to do. I'm unmaking your war, Brainard. I'm countermanding your orders and tearing up your plans. I'm making peace! [*A silence.*]

BRAINARD. Peace! Is it peace, or surrender? Is it truce or treason? That a President of the United States should take a stand so *cowardly*. . . .

GORDON. Oh, no. You left me in no position for a

coward. It was easy enough for you to get us *into* this, Brainard. But making peace is harder than making war.

BRAINARD. Go through with it, then!

GORDON. That's easy, too. But I'm choosing another way, the right way, even if I have to go it alone.

BRAINARD. Alone!

GORDON. If I thought I *could!*

FITZGERALD. We know that! You don't *want* help!

BRIGHT. We've offered to co-operate—it's no use.

BRAINARD. You can't afford to lose these men, Mr. President. I know something about your position. Even for your own ambitious ideas, you're helpless without support.

GORDON. I won't compromise.

BRAINARD [*angrily*]. What else do you call it—crippling the nation's defences, preaching arbitration! What are you going to do? You must have *something* in mind!

GORDON. Give me time. We've fought wars for thousands of years. But there's a way. . . .

BRAINARD. What is it?—Manila's taken, and you withdraw the fleet. A thousand men killed, and you send regrets to the enemy. What more are you going to do? Haul down the colors at home, cede California to the Japs, surrender the Capitol to the enemy . . . ! Why don't you make a complete job of it, Gordon? Why not go to Japan, and hand over your sword personally to the Emperor! . . .

FITZGERALD. Yes! *Go to Japan. . . .*

BRAINARD. Go to Tokio, and lick the dirt . . . ! [GORDON *is silent.*] Well?

WILMOT. This isn't getting us anywhere!

BRIGHT. Mr. Brainard, it's no use. You can't reason with him.

WILMOT. It's all right to talk, but we've accomplished nothing. We've stated our demands, and the President's got no answer! The meeting is over——

GORDON [*to* DUNCAN]. Call Admiral James.

DUNCAN. Admiral James, sir?

GORDON. Yes, bring him here.

DUNCAN. Yes, sir. [*Exits.*]

GORDON. Perhaps we can put one of his ships to some use. You say we're at war, yet none of us knows the country or people we're fighting. They're as unreal as Mme Butterfly. It's time we had a ship at Yokohama without music. Mr. Wilmot, how long does it take to span the Pacific?

WILMOT. Ask the Navy Department.

GORDON. I will. Turner, get me the Navy Depart-partment.

TURNER. Yes, sir.

HILL. We haven't time for this nonsense. Are you coming, Bright?

GORDON. Mr. Fitzgerald, have you ever been to Japan?

FITZGERALD. What? Certainly not!

GORDON. Miss Folwell, would you like to go to Japan?

FOLWELL. When do we start, Mr. President?

GORDON. That's the first helpful reply I've had. —When do planes leave for the coast, Mr. Dickinson? Miss Folwell, charter me a plane for San Francisco.

FOLWELL. Yes, Mr. President. [*Exits.*]

TURNER. Here's the Navy Department.

GORDON. I don't want them any more. Get me Mrs. Gordon.

BRIGHT. Are you proposing, Mr. President, in this crisis, to leave the country?

GORDON. I'm not proposing.—I'm deciding. You asked me how I would wage war if I didn't fight. Well, I've found the way—thanks to my honored predecessor, Mr. Brainard. I shall wage war by starting at the end instead of at the beginning. I'll go to Tokio for my peace conference before, instead of after, the fighting.

BRIGHT. I warn you, this means impeachment.

FITZGERALD. There isn't time for impeachment. I demand the President's resignation.

GORDON. Refused. I shan't resign. I can't. I'm

too busy. I'm going to Japan, and I'm sailing to-night.

[*General confusion and dismay.*]

CURTAIN

ACT THREE

ACT THREE

SCENE I

[*Tokio. An anteroom outside* PRESIDENT GORDON'S *suite in the hotel. Two weeks after Act II. Late afternoon.* TURNER *is seated on sofa; in front of him a small table with bottles and glasses.* DUNCAN *is standing at window, left.* MISS FOLWELL *is pacing restlessly up and down.* TODU *enters through door at rear, walks to water cooler on table at right, pours and drinks a glass of water, turns and exits.*]

TURNER. God! These Japs! Are we never going to get any news from in there?

FOLWELL. [*Looking at the door of the conference room.*] No news is good news.

TURNER. I suppose when Lindbergh flew the Atlantic, no news was good news. When President Gordon is in there [*pointing to the door*] begging for a chance to meet with the Premier of Japan, no news is good news.

FOLWELL. It's got to be good news.

TURNER. You mean you think that Lord Carrington is going to be able to persuade those Japanese nabobs that Prince Yato must receive the President? You're crazy!

DUNCAN. They must be *listening* to him! They've been in there two hours.

TURNER. Oh! This international world series! The President makes a grandstand play by coming to Japan. Score one for America! The Japanese Premier refuses to see him, and politely offers a flag of truce and safe-conduct home. Score one for Japan! The British Ambassador intervenes, insists on a conference, and if he succeeds, it will be score two for America. And here I sit! Dr. Fujimoto arrives at five. No news! At five-twenty that Jap with the poker face comes out for a drink of water. No news! At five-thirty Baron Ishiwara leaves. No news! At six-ten, out comes poker-face again, for more water. All water—no news! If a preliminary discussion takes as long as this, the main bout will outlast the war. [*A pause.*] Stop walking, Folwell. You make me nervous. Sit down and have a hari-kari. [*Offers her a drink.*]

FOLWELL. [*Goes to the door.*] No, thank you!

TURNER. Come away from that door. You can't hear anything. These Japanese automatons whisper—they don't *talk*. [FOLWELL *joins* DUNCAN *at the window.*] And come away from that window. Somebody will be taking a pot-shot at you.

FOLWELL. [*Indignant.*] You've got pot-shots on the brain. You were sure somebody was going to fire at the President on his way from Yokohama yesterday. But no one did. If you're losing your nerve, Turner, you'd better go back to your room, and hide your head in a pillow.

TURNER. I'm not losing my nerve, old girl. I just don't like kidding myself. Don't forget that America has declared war! You're at *war* with that crowd out there.

FOLWELL. Funny! I don't feel even mad at them. And they don't look very belligerent. They seem quite busy discussing things.

DUNCAN. It looks like Columbus Circle on election night. [*Sound of drums and tramp of passing soldiers.*]

TURNER. Well, I guess that sounds belligerent. More troops passing.

FOLWELL. But no cheering, you note! [*Sudden cheers.*]

TURNER. No cheering, eh? The goose-step gets them every time!

[*Enter* TODU, *who goes to water cooler, takes a drink, and starts to exit.*]

TURNER. [*Sings.*] Water Boy!!!

DUNCAN. [*Stopping him.*] Mr. Todu, if you don't

mind. Has General Nogatu agreed to the conference tomorrow?

TODU. Mr. Duncan, your servant. When the meeting is finished, you will be at liberty to inquire the details of Mr. President Gordon.

DUNCAN. Of course. Thank you.

TODU. Thank you!

DUNCAN. It would help, if you could give us some idea——

TODU. War has been declared, Mr. Duncan. I no longer have ideas. With your honorable permission—— [*He bows, and goes inside.*]

TURNER. Same to you, if you'll pardon my Japanese.

FOLWELL. Well, what do you make of that?

DUNCAN. [*A bit quizzically.*] That it might be a good plan to accept Lord Carrington's offer of a guard!

TURNER. [*Somewhat more than a bit disgusted.*] That it might be a better plan to accept Prince Yato's offer of a flag of truce to take us home!

FOLWELL. Oh, you make me tired.

TURNER. War declared, the Cabinet busted, the Senate ready to impeach the President before you can say "Senator Bright"——

FOLWELL. When do we get the next bulletin from home?

DUNCAN. It will be just like the last one. "Impeachment resolution before Senate tomorrow." How long does it take a senator to make up his mind?

FOLWELL. Longer than a representative. He has to think!

TURNER. The President hasn't got a Chinaman's chance.

FOLWELL. Who says he hasn't? Why don't you keep quiet if you can't talk sense?

TURNER. What's the matter, Folwell? *You* losing your nerve? Well, I don't wonder—caught here like rats in a trap! This is the biggest fool's errand since the Ford Peace ship. Five idealists, pretending that one man, all alone, can talk Japan out of war.

FOLWELL. He's not alone. There are hundreds of that crowd who are with him. You heard them cheering him yesterday.

TURNER. And cheering the army today!

DUNCAN. *Koyé's* followers weren't cheering the army.

TURNER. Koyé's in jail—and most of his followers, too.

DUNCAN. Oh, you think so! Come here a minute, if you're not afraid of pot-shots. See those policemen breaking up that group!

TURNER. [*Going to the window.*] Sure.

DUNCAN. If you will watch the way that group disperses, you will see that they merely move into a wider circle, and then gradually reassemble in another place.

TURNER. All Japs look alike to me.

DUNCAN. Watch them carefully, now. That group over there! See?—That's trained resistance to the police, like strikers on a picket-line.

TURNER. You call this a strike?

DUNCAN. [*Paying no attention.*] Folwell, did you notice anything peculiar about those troops that scared Turner just now?

FOLWELL. I can't say that I did.

DUNCAN. Well, I did. The inside files of the whole company were unarmed.

TURNER. Oh, come now! You don't think they're running out of munitions.

DUNCAN. *Those soldiers were under arrest!*

TURNER. [*Impressed, in spite of himself.*] You're not trying to sell me a tale of mutiny, Duncan?

DUNCAN. Why not? Perhaps that's the news you're looking for!

[*A knock on door at right. They all turn, in surprise.*]

DUNCAN. Come in!

[*There is no answer.* DUNCAN *crosses to the door, and opens it. A Japanese* BELL-GIRL, *in hotel uniform, enters with a folded news-*

paper in her hand. She is all smiles and curtsies. Speaks in very broken English.]

BELL-GIRL. If—you—please—— [*Holds out the newspaper.*]

DUNCAN. What is this?

BELL-GIRL. If—you—please!—— [*Pointing to newspaper.*] This—for—*here!*

[DUNCAN *takes the paper mechanically. Before he can speak again, the* GIRL *bows, exits, and closes the door.*]

DUNCAN. That's peculiar!

TURNER. Well, a newspaper is a *newspaper!* [*Snatches the paper, and sits down on the sofa. He looks at the paper expectantly, then groans.*] Oh, of course! *In Japanese!* What good is that?

FOLWELL. Read it from top to bottom, instead of from left to right.

DUNCAN. Sure, that's the idea!

TURNER. Wait a minute! Here's some English—*figures! Stock reports!* [*Starts rattling off quotations.*] "U. S. Steel 70 down to 50; Jennings Steel 130 down to 110; poor old Wilmot——

DUNCAN [*impatiently*]. Quit your kidding, Turner!

TURNER. On my honor—look! [*Holds out the paper. He opens it quickly, and an envelope tumbles out.* DUNCAN *sees it, and picks it up.*]

DUNCAN. What's this?

FOLWELL. Addressed to President Gordon!

[*As they gather in a cluster, to see the envelope, the door rear is opened by* TODU. *Enter* NOGATU, *in military uniform, and* DR. FUJIMOTO *in native robes.*]

DUNCAN. Ah, General Nogatu—Dr. Fujimoto. [*Bows.*]

NOGATU. Mr. Duncan!

[*They bow, and cross stage to door at right, where they pause.*]

NOGATU. [*To* FUJIMOTO *in Japanese.*] (That's all right!)

FUJIMOTO. (Tomorrow there will be no difficulty.)

NOGATU. (Not if Yato stands firm.)

[*As they exit,* GORDON *enters. He seems elated, and assured.*]

DUNCAN. Well, Mr. President?

GORDON. [*Rubbing his hands.*] It's all right. The conference has been granted.

FOLWELL. That's splendid, sir.

TURNER. That's great——

GORDON. I meet Yato tomorrow morning at eleven. Dickinson will give you the arrangements.

FOLWELL. We congratulate you, Mr. President. —It's such a relief——

GORDON. And thank Lord Carrington! His intervention tipped the scales. He was magnificent. [*To* DUNCAN.] Have you had any word?

DUNCAN. Nothing, sir.

GORDON [*thoughtfully*]. I see. . . . Well— [*Looks at the three.*] If I am impeached——

FOLWELL. Mr. Gordon!

GORDON. As seems very likely—it will make a great difference. I shall be a mere private citizen, with no authority. [*To* TURNER.] Turner, you'd better go down to wait for the message.

TURNER. Yes, sir! Hopkins is on duty till I return.

GORDON [*to* FOLWELL]. Miss Folwell, I have a special order for you. Go get some rest! You've been at it steadily for two weeks. You need sleep.

FOLWELL. Thank you, but I have too much to do.

GORDON. We can't do anything more now.

FOLWELL. I couldn't rest. Please let me stay.—I must *know*—— [*She stops, and seems about to cry.*]

GORDON [*very gently*]. I'll need you to look your very best, tomorrow. I'm counting on it.—Go get some rest.—Executive order!

FOLWELL. [*Resigned, and again composed.*] If I *must*, Mr. President. [*Exits.*]

GORDON [*to* DUNCAN]. You'd better get some rest, too.

DUNCAN. Yes, sir.

GORDON. You're just next door.—I'll knock if I need you.—There's nothing more, now?

DUNCAN. Yes, Mr. President, if you will pardon me. This note! [*Hands envelope to* GORDON, *who opens, and reads from a rough scrap of paper. Looks up, puzzled.*]

GORDON. Where did you get this?

DUNCAN. It dropped out of a newspaper which a bell-girl just brought here.

[*The shouts of the crowd rise outside.*]

GORDON. It's a message—of some kind.

DUNCAN. From whom, sir?

GORDON. [*Turning the paper over.*] I don't know. It's unsigned. Apparently from somebody outside. It reads like a Delphic oracle. [*Reads from the paper.*] "The furrows have been turned, and the seed sown. The brave man trusts in the harvest."

[*Enter* DICKINSON *and* LORD CARRINGTON *through door at rear.* GORDON *glances up.*]

DUNCAN. Oh, Lord Carrington, thank you so much for your help.

CARRINGTON. It was a privilege.

DUNCAN. Thank you, sir. [*To* GORDON.] Is that all for now?

GORDON. That's all, thank you. [DUNCAN *and* TURNER *exit.*] How can I thank you, Lord Carrington. You have saved me from shipwreck at the very start.

CARRINGTON. I was fortunate in having the instructions of my government. When London ordered me to support your request for a conference, in the general interest of mankind—for we're all involved, you know—there was nothing for Japan to do but yield.

GORDON. It didn't seem so, for a while. But your personal appeal, Mr. Ambassador——

CARRINGTON [*quickly*]. And yours, sir!

DICKINSON. I believe Your Excellency enjoys risking your neck for a sporting proposition.

CARRINGTON. Oh, I'm in no danger here. I've been in Tokio longer than the Emperor.

[DICKINSON *offers* CARRINGTON *a drink.*]

CARRINGTON. Thank you. [*Laughs, starts to go.*] Well, good luck tomorrow! [*Drinks with* DICKINSON. *Then, solemnly.*] And we'll need it! [*Turns to* GORDON.] You've got yourself into a pretty bad hole, Mr. President. For God's sake, see that you get out of it. I must warn you not to be deceived. This was only a skirmish this morning—the real battle comes tomorrow. Prince Yato was what you Americans call "sitting pretty" when he refused to see you. You would have had to return to America, with your mission a complete failure. Then, unexpectedly, my government forced his hand—also humiliated him before his people. He's had to back down, and that means he's got to regain his prestige. Mr. President, our success this afternoon was too complete. To be frank with you, I suspect a trap—some trick which these Japanese will turn to their own advantage. Look out for a move that may surprise us!

GORDON. I must take my chances on that.

DICKINSON. The President has realized from the beginning that he is facing a gamble.

GORDON. Not so great a gamble as war! In any case, your presence at the conference table, Lord Carrington, will be an invaluable service.

CARRINGTON. But there are limits to what we can do. My government went about as far today as it can go. My presence tomorrow will be hardly more than that of a friendly observer. You must settle things, single-handed, with Yato and Nogatu—and they're dangerous!

DICKINSON. You know, Lord Carrington, I was opposed to this venture. I am here purely out of loyalty to my chief. It was a relief yesterday to see public sentiment so largely on his side. The people seem not unfriendly.

CARRINGTON. Well, of course, there is the phenomenon we diplomats have a way of forgetting. The chemical action of public opinion! There's been a good deal of peace sentiment here for a long time. But don't trust that crowd. It's the government you have to deal with tomorrow. Of course your coming here certainly placed Yato in an uncomfortable position. He's been going along with Nogatu and the militarists. And you come, and demoralize his war-drive!

GORDON. That's what I hoped to do!

CARRINGTON. Yato and his counsellors were utterly mystified by what you did. They knew how to deal with battleships, but they didn't know what in thunder to do with President Gordon.

DICKINSON. One man——

CARRINGTON [*exultantly*]. The sailing of that single unarmed ship into the war-zone was more costly to them than the loss of a fleet at sea. [*Suddenly stern.*] But now, Mr. President, they propose to have a victory—all the more as we outwitted them in this initial encounter.

GORDON. There is no question of victory, Lord Carrington. I am here to make peace.

CARRINGTON. You are facing an enemy at bay, Mr. President. The sword is out of the sheath. I could almost wish, Gordon, for your own sake, that you had accepted Yato's safe-conduct home, under that flag of truce.

GORDON. [*Aroused again.*] Impossible! You

yourself have pointed out the humiliation—and defeat!

CARRINGTON. Yes, yes—forgive me! But you are in danger—physical danger! Let us protect you with a guard.

GORDON. I'm sorry, Lord Carrington.

CARRINGTON. At least Secret Service protection. No one need know.

GORDON. Thank you, Lord Carrington, but I cannot sue for peace with a gun in my hand. I trust my enemy. That is my only strength.

CARRINGTON. Very well—— [CARRINGTON *looks at* DICKINSON, *and shakes his head.*]

DICKINSON. You're sure of yourself, Gordon.

GORDON. I must be. [*To* CARRINGTON.] Until tomorrow.

[DICKINSON *hesitates, then holds out his hand. Enter* DUNCAN *hurriedly, carrying a message.*]

GORDON. What is it, Duncan?

DUNCAN. [*Reading.*] The Senate has convened, Mr. President, to take its final *vote on your impeachment.* [*He hands the message to* GORDON.]

CURTAIN

Scene II

[*Tokio. A conference chamber. Noon, the next day.* GORDON, DICKINSON, CARRINGTON *are seated left center.* DUNCAN *and* MISS FOLWELL *left of them.* PRINCE YATO, DR. FUJIMOTO, GENERAL NOGATU, BARON ISHIWARA *are seated right center.* JAPANESE SECRETARIES *sit at a desk down right.* TODU *stands. A loud murmur and shouts from the crowd outside.*]

CARRINGTON. Prince Yato. Gentlemen. The President of the United States has asked me to act as intermediary in this extraordinary session brought about in the interest of peace between your two countries. He wishes me, first of all, to apologize for his unfamiliarity with your language, and to thank you for your willingness to use his. I hope we may have a frank and open discussion of the question at hand: the settlement of disputes between the Japanese Empire and the United States. General Nogatu, Dr. Fujimoto and I have spoken with President Gordon privately, and know his position. I should like him to present it to you.—Mr. President. [CARRINGTON *sits down.*]

GORDON. Lord Carrington, Mr. Premier, as President of the United States, I have undertaken an unusual mission in the confidence that I might find, with your help, a common ground on which to settle our grievance without bloodshed. I did this in the full knowledge that it was a new procedure, knowing also that only desperate measures could prevent a more desperate conflict. I count on your discretion.

YATO. [*Pause.*] Mr. President . . . I must reply by being frank with you. We do not know, my colleagues nor I, *why* you have come to our country.

GORDON. Is it unusual, Mr. Premier, for the head of one nation to visit that of another?

YATO. Not at all. I have myself visited your country. But not in a state of war.

GORDON. Because of this state of war I am here.

YATO. For that very reason you should not be here.

GORDON. I have come to end this state of war.

YATO. War can be ended in only one way. By victory and defeat, in battle.

GORDON. Pardon me, Mr. Premier. It can be ended by the agreement of governments, before victory and defeat have stirred up the hatred that makes agreement impossible.

YATO. Your country has already acted . . .

GORDON. Without my recognition nor sanction.

YATO. That is a matter for you to settle. Your country has declared war without provocation.

DICKINSON [*interrupting*]. —After your forces attacked Manila . . . !

CARRINGTON. Mr. Dickinson, if you please. . . .

YATO. What motivated that attack? *Your* ultimatum. *Your* fleet manœuvres.

GORDON. I admit that. [*Pause.*] This is the first point on which we agree.

YATO. You admit a state of war. Why do you refuse to wage it?

GORDON. Because I do not believe in war.

YATO. You do not move your armies nor your fleet. You come here, instead, on a mysterious mission.

GORDON. There is nothing mysterious, Mr. Premier. We are not playing the game of war. That is all.

YATO. I am not sure.

[DR. FUJIMOTO *asks a question, in Japanese.* YATO *repeats* GORDON'S *statement. They smile.* ISHIWARA *and* FUJIMOTO *confer. Ad lib. in Japanese.*]

GORDON. How can I make you sure, Prince Yato? —I ask for your confidence.

YATO. You do not *dare* to fight.

GORDON. Mr. Premier, we are not here to discover

new grievances, nor suspicions. We are here to prevent a catastrophe! [*Pause.*] I have come to Tokio at the risk of my office, my reputation, perhaps my life, to stop the war while there is still time.

YATO. You should have thought of that weeks ago, when your President sent the ultimatum to our Emperor.

GORDON. Must we continue to discuss what happened before I assumed office?—I refuse to recognize that ultimatum. I have withdrawn the fleet. I ask you now to risk as much. [YATO *is silent.*] I simply believe that neither of our nations wants war. I have confidence in my own people, as I have in the people of Japan. [*Pause.*] Lord Carrington, will you explain that to the delegates, please?

CARRINGTON. [*Speaks in Japanese.*] (The President does not believe that either nation wants war.)

FUJIMOTO. (America started the war, we cannot help it.)

CARRINGTON. He says America, it's quite evident, started the war, and they can't help it.

YATO. You are here, Mr. President, to take advantage of your high office by watching us, to see what we shall do. You have come to delay our preparations for war. We are ready; you are not! Meanwhile, in America, you *make* ready . . . !

DICKINSON. This is uncalled-for, Mr. Premier! You cannot believe . . .

YATO. You come to mislead our people, to stir up the enemies of our government. You teach the people that you are their friend, and we are their enemies—and they *protest* against the war. You make us courtesies, and all the time, you stab us in the back.

CARRINGTON. Prince Yato. The President of an enemy nation has crossed the sea, in time of war, at great personal danger to himself, to seek understanding with you. He is the *guest* of Japan . . .

YATO. Uninvited!

CARRINGTON. Nevertheless, President Gordon is here, in your hands.

YATO. Yes. He is in our hands. And he believes, as you do, that my government will not dare to act against him. [*Pause.*] Mr. Ambassador, you are a statesman. You do not imagine that we can let the President come to Japan with his aides, see, and hear—and then go home?—Mr. President, you will not be permitted to confuse my people indefinitely. [*He takes up the document from the table.*] We have here, Mr. Secretary of State, our terms of peace.

DICKINSON. [*Eagerly taking them.*] At last! Something definite . . . !

[DICKINSON *shares the document with* GORDON. *After a pause.*]

GORDON. Terms of peace, Mr. Premier—or terms of surrender?

YATO. I am glad that you understand, Mr. President.

GORDON. [*Taking document from* DICKINSON, *lays it down.*] I am not here to ask terms. Least of all to surrender.

YATO [*angrily*]. It is surrender—or *fight!*

GORDON. I recognize no such alternative.

YATO. [*Pause. Rise.*] Very well, Mr. President. —I believe this conference is at an end.

[*All the Japanese rise.* YATO *turns to his colleagues.*]

CARRINGTON. [*Rises.*] Prince Yato, may I beg you, in the interest of your country, as well as President Gordon's . . . ?

YATO. I should be a traitor to my country, if I did not fight the enemy when I meet him. The President has refused open warfare. He has insisted instead upon meeting us in conference. The terms offered by me he rejects.—My duty is clear.

CARRINGTON. The President comes trusting in your generosity, your good-will, your love of justice . . .

YATO. In war, Mr. Ambassador, there is no generosity, no good-will, no love of justice. There is only power, force. In war we strike, to win! [*Turns abruptly to* NOGATU *and speaks in Japanese.*] (Arrest him.)

NOGATU. Mr. President, in the name of His Sacred Majesty, the Emperor, I order your *arrest*, as prisoner of war. Todu! [TODU *salutes.*] (Get the soldiers.)

[GORDON *rises, steps back.* TODU *exits and calls command to soldiers.*]

DICKINSON. Arrest? Mr. Premier, this is incredible!

YATO. I am sorry to disagree.

DICKINSON. One moment, Mr. Premier.—General Nogatu! [*Pause.*] If you go through with this arrest, you will be signing your own political death warrant. Your government will fall . . . !

YATO. I am not an idealist, Mr. Secretary. Only a servant of my country. What happens to me or my cabinet does not matter——

[*Soldiers enter.*]

CARRINGTON. [*Goes to* YATO, *as* GORDON *confers with* DUNCAN *and* DICKINSON.] Mr. Premier, I must, of course, send word of this at once to London.

YATO [*defiantly*]. Yes, to London.—To Berlin and Paris. Let them all hear. The day has passed when Japan was to be frightened by the West.—

Have you any further business, Mr. Ambassador? [*Long pause.*] If not, I must proceed with mine. [*Turns to* GORDON.] It is with regret, Mr. President . . . !

DICKINSON. Wait a minute! Are you sure that he *is* the President! . . . [DICKINSON *crosses to* YATO.] Are you so sure? President Gordon is on trial at this moment, before his own Congress. This very morning we may hear that he has been convicted of the crime of trying to make peace for his country.

CARRINGTON. Quite true, Mr. Dickinson! [*To* YATO.] If the President is impeached, you will have in your hands not the head of a great nation, but a private citizen of as much significance to you as some sentry caught off guard.

YATO. As you suggest, gentlemen. In that case, we need not consider the respect due the President of a foreign power. I shall see that our prisoner receives all the attentions usually accorded—a sentry caught off guard!

[*General consternation among the American contingent.*]

CARRINGTON. Be careful that you don't go too far . . . !

YATO. Are you speaking as Ambassador or as an arbitrator, Lord Carrington?

CARRINGTON. As an Englishman. My sovereign would like to see peace among the nations. In his name I protest this act as a high-handed, militaristic threat which will only succeed in involving *all* of us in war.

YATO [*menacingly*]. Mr. Ambassador, you will stop this insulting interference. Otherwise . . . !

CARRINGTON. Do you threaten *me* with arrest? You wouldn't dare . . .

YATO. Try me and see. [*Pause.* YATO *and* NOGATU *confer.*]

GORDON [*coming forward*]. Thank you, Lord Carrington. You are very kind. [CARRINGTON *pauses, then returns to his chair.*] Mr. Premier . . . I should like to ask you, as one *man* to another, what you hope to gain by detaining me.

YATO. I am Premier of Japan. I cannot step down from my office.

GORDON. Then perhaps you will listen to one who still has that privilege.—What have you to gain?

YATO. What have I to lose?

GORDON. War! The incalculable loss of war! [*He begins to speak now like a man possessed.*] More terrible than earthquake and famine! Prince Yato, you know something about these horrors —your country swept with ruin, your people dead by the thousands! We have helped you when you were thus helpless before the forces of nature—mourned with you for these lives you could not save. But would you not have saved them, if you *could?* Had it been in your power, as it is now with this war, would you not have stayed disaster before you lost everything?

YATO. We shall not lose the war.

GORDON. Wars are always lost. Victor and vanquished alike, lose everything.—Wealth, trade, productive enterprise, security, your progress through half a century——

YATO. And we gain?

GORDON. Nothing! A mile or two of territory, a huge debt, millions of discontented citizens, the contempt of the world, the curse of history. Weigh *these* against the lives of your young men —millions of them—boys who love life . . .

YATO. Who love Japan, and will gladly die for her!

GORDON. At your order! Mr. Premier, by what right do you give that order?

YATO. The right of my great office, as Minister of His Most Sacred Majesty, the Emperor, Guardian of his Person, Protector of his Honor; the proud tradition of the Samurai which binds us in loyalty to our Sovereign. For thirty centuries we have stood watch about his throne, as stars about the sun, and have not failed; His hand, which touches us as it has touched our fathers, ordains us Servants of the Will of Heaven. This is my right!

GORDON [*quietly, to* YATO]. Mr. Premier, I revere

your traditions. But you not only serve your Emperor. You administer as well a modern state. Under the laws of your country, as of mine, murder is a crime. Not even you, Mr. Premier, can take so much as a single life with your own hands. Go out upon these crowded streets. Pick out the meanest beggar in all that multitude of people. Kill him as you would vermin—and you will be guilty of a capital offense. [*With rising emphasis.*] Yet by the stroke of a pen, the whisper of a word, you would send a million of your fairest men to death in battle—and call it glory! What is this myth of war that makes wholesale murder beautiful? Under the sanction of what law, on the tables of what religion, is it written that you may kill, not with disgrace but with honor, if only you kill a million, and not one? [*Pause.*] And remember this, to a million of your countrymen dead you must add a million of mine dead. For soldiers die—but before they die, they *kill.*

YATO. Yet you declared this war.

GORDON. [*With tremendous vehemence.*] No! Never! Madmen in my country declared the war, as madmen in your country provoked it, and as madmen in both countries will fight it.—I have come, Mr. Premier, to stop this war.

YATO. It is too late.

GORDON. It is never too late. Not for those people who are praying for peace.

YATO. There is no way . . . [*He is obviously beginning to be troubled by* GORDON'S *plea.*]

GORDON. There *is* a way! When we began our disputes, months ago, there were two paths before us. There always are—paths that divide. We took the path of arrogance and force. The other is still open. Mr. Premier, I have come to take that path—the path of reason. As a practical man, Prince Yato, a statesman who would serve the interests of my country, and of yours, I insist that we make peace—today, when we may both be victors, instead of tomorrow when we shall both lie broken and defeated.

[TURNER *enters, hurriedly, and goes to* MISS FOLWELL, *and delivers message. During succeeding speech, she hands it to* DUNCAN, *who passes it to* DICKINSON.]

YATO. You are an eloquent man, Mr. Gordon. Your thoughts are great thoughts. Confucius had them. Buddha founded a religion on them. But I am statesman in authority and must deal with statesmen in authority. This conference, Mr. President, is at an end.

CARRINGTON. Mr. Premier, I must insist . . .

YATO. I have listened too long. [*Turns to* GOR-

DON, *as* CARRINGTON *is handed dispatch by* DICKINSON.] As a prisoner of war, I am forced to place you in the hands of General Nogatu.

CARRINGTON. But Mr. Premier . . .

YATO. The conference, Mr. Ambassador, is ended.

CARRINGTON. [*With splendid assurance.*] The conference, Prince Yato, is *not* ended. [*Indicating message.*] The impeachment trial of President Gordon has been suspended in the United States Senate, pending the outcome of peace negotiations with Japan.

GORDON. Suspended sentence! [*Shakes hands with* DUNCAN. *General excitement.* GORDON *and Americans confer.*]

CARRINGTON. Mr. Premier, you know what this means! President Gordon has won his fight at home. Public opinion has forced the Senate to suspend action. The American people are with him. He speaks now not for himself, but for his country.

NOGATU. [*Intervening sharply, as* YATO *hesitates as though in confusion.*] Yes, Mr. Ambassador —for his country! The head of a great nation. As our prisoner . . .

CARRINGTON. [*Aghast.*] Prisoner? Now?

NOGATU. [*As* YATO *starts to interrupt.*] Yes, we will hold him as hostage for his country.

DICKINSON. You don't propose to hold the President prisoner—in the face of this dispatch?

[DICKINSON *takes dispatch from* CARRINGTON'S *hand. As he does so, altercation breaks out between* YATO *and* NOGATU. YATO *is obviously troubled,* NOGATU *excited and violent. They speak together in Japanese, as* GORDON, CARRINGTON *and* DICKINSON *look on in amazement.*]

YATO. [*Speaking in Japanese.*] (We must be careful, General. Lord Carrington is right—this news changes the situation. We must wait—consider . . .)

NOGATU. (No, never! If the situation is changed, it is only to hurry matters. Action is now imperative.)

YATO. (I shall not hurry matters. That would be fatal. Who knows what will happen when this news is known?)

CARRINGTON. [*Who has been listening intently, translates and thus explains to* GORDON.] Prince Yato is troubled. He is worried about the people when they hear about this dispatch.

NOGATU. [*Continuing, in Japanese, to* YATO.] (It will be fatal only to wait. The public must know nothing until Gordon's arrest has been announced. There is no time to be lost.)

YATO. (Silence, Nogatu. I am in authority here.)

[*As the two men thus contend, now in open anger,* CARRINGTON *turns again and speaks quietly to* GORDON.]

CARRINGTON. The Japanese front is breaking, Mr. President. Your enemies are at war not with you, but with one another.

[NOGATU, *overborne by* YATO, *is silent. He turns away in sullen anger.*]

YATO. Mr. President, Lord Carrington, it is obvious that a new factor has entered into this situation . . .

CARRINGTON. I thought you'd realize that, Mr. Premier.

[*He is interrupted by a wild, ecstatic shout from without. The crowds are in sudden pandemonium. All look toward the windows.*]

FOLWELL. [*Jumping up.*] The people have heard the news!

DUNCAN. Turner saw to that!

CARRINGTON. [*Turning to* YATO.] Mr. Premier, the people seem to have heard the news that we have heard. [*Cheers rise and fall.*] Listen to those cheers. You cannot take this nation into war.

GORDON. [*Conciliatory, as always.*] There is no war between us, Prince Yato. Our people, yours and mine, now stand together.

YATO. I cannot agree, Mr. President. A few wild shouts . . . [*The telephone rings.* YATO *answers it. Speaks in Japanese.*] (Hello!) [*The shouts become a roar. Cries of "Koyé."*]

TURNER. What's happening over there?

DUNCAN. I can't see. There's some new disturbance in the crowd.

FOLWELL. Look at that mass of people crowding through the square.

[YATO *leaves the telephone and speaks, in Japanese, to* TODU.]

YATO. (They're storming the jail—shouting for Koyé. Quick! Find out what's happening.)

[*Exit* TODU.]

CARRINGTON. Mr. President, news has come through. The crowd has stormed the jail.

TURNER. What's that they're shouting?

DUNCAN. Sounds like "Koyé."

TURNER. Yes, that's it. Listen to them.

FOLWELL. Mr. President, that crowd is shouting for Koyé!

TURNER. Duncan, do you see what I see? Mr. President, do you see that fellow they're carrying on their shoulders?

DUNCAN. Folwell, come here and look. They're carrying some man!

YATO. Mr. Secretary—that dispatch, if you please! We have not yet been notified! [*To* FUJIMOTO.] (Confirm that.)

CARRINGTON [*at the window*]. They've released Koyé.

TURNER. That must be he they're carrying through the streets.

NOGATU. (Arrest the President.)

YATO. (No, Nogatu, we can't do that.)

NOGATU. (I know my duty.)

YATO. (Silence, or I shall place you under arrest.)

CARRINGTON. Nogatu is defying his chief.

NOGATU. (I'm going to take him to jail.)

YATO. (Don't be a fool.) Mr. President, in this emergency the conference will be adjourned.

NOGATU. No! No! In this emergency, the *army* will take control!

[TODU *enters.*]

TODU. [*Speaking in Japanese.*] (Prince Yato, Koyé is free! They broke the jail!)

YATO. (We know that.)

NOGATU. (What are the troops doing?)

TODU. (The soldiers will not fire on the crowd.)

CARRINGTON. [*With frenzied exultation.*] Mr. President, the soldiers have refused to fire on the crowd. Koyé is free.

DICKINSON. Good God, this is revolution.

CARRINGTON [*at the window*]. Koyé is *here!*

YATO. [*In desperate confusion.*] Mr. President, this conference must stand adjourned—until tomorrow.

GORDON. Prince Yato, we cannot wait. Your people are demanding peace.

YATO. My people! That rabble!

[*A sudden sound of wild cheering, with rush of feet, without. The crowd is loose, and making for the hotel. The tumult draws quickly nearer. There comes a fierce pounding at the doors, which at last break open. A vast crowd of men and women, in native costume, accompanied by soldiers who have thrown down their arms, sweeps into the room. The Japanese counsellors are swept aside. At the height of the turmoil enters* KOYÉ, *a majestic figure, in tattered prison garb, his chest bare. He is very calm. He walks slowly to* GORDON.]

KOYÉ. Mr. President. I come to welcome you in the name of my people, and to claim you as a leader.

GORDON. Koyé!

KOYÉ. We were called to fight against your people. We did not want to fight. What quarrel had we? We were happy in our homes, and on our farms. What do we ask—only to be let alone!

GORDON. As people everywhere want to be left alone!

KOYÉ. But what could we do? We were not strong. We were beaten, crushed, we had failed. Then suddenly, Mr. President, as a spark from tinder, the miracle flashed across the sea. You were coming to Japan! In a day, the word had gone to every corner of the land, like the wind rustling the leaves of a forest. No village so remote it did not hear—no man so humble he did not understand. *President Gordon coming to Japan to ask for peace!* At that moment, Mr. President, as though the heavens had spoken, war became impossible. Your coming was the sound of gongs before our altars. Your presence more terrible than an army with banners. We knew that America wanted peace and would bring us peace. We saw a friendly host reaching out their hands in brotherhood. We were glad, and suddenly we were brave!

NOGATU [*in Japanese*]. (Treason! Treason!)

KOYÉ. Yes, General, treason if you will. It is nothing new, the call of *liberty is as old as the world.* Listen to it, or are you so old in the ways of war that you are deaf to the people when they call for peace?

NOGATU. (Peace!)

KOYÉ. We played fair, General. We gave you your chance. But the moment you gave the order for my arrest, I knew—the people knew—we were stronger than we had dared to hope. With America we were your masters . . .

NOGATU. (Masters!)

KOYÉ. What a fool you were to make me a martyr to this cause. See! See! [*Holds out his hands and arms, bleeding.*] These scars! *They* have beaten you. My chains have made us free. [NOGATU, *like a furious animal, makes a sudden move—dashes at* KOYÉ. *The two men stand face to face for a moment. Then* NOGATU *backs away, as though dazzled and afraid. Then forgetting everything he calls for guards—gives orders, as though in command.* KOYÉ, *with superb serenity and quiet, continues.*] No, General, you have no guards. [NOGATU *looks around as though in amazement.*] What need we of guards? The people now rule themselves—and you. [NOGATU, *with a hoarse and angry cry, rushes to the door.*] You are free to go, Nogatu. But where will you go? Everywhere you will find the people. On the streets, through the city, in the highways and in the villages, to the slopes of Fujiyama—only the people! They will not hurt you—but neither will they heed you! [*Majestically yet pitifully.*] Poor fool, your day is done!

[NOGATU *crumples, baffled and beaten. A messenger enters and speaks to* YATO.]

GORDON. You are a brave man, Koyé. I salute you!

KOYÉ. [*Steps to* GORDON.] A common man! But you are President Gordon. Your faith gave me opportunity, your courage brought me strength. Without you, I would be crying to the stars, unheard. [*Firmly.*] Mr. President—you came for peace, and we bring you peace.

GORDON. It is your voice, Koyé, that I have waited all these years to hear.

KOYÉ. And I, yours!

YATO. [*Stepping forward.*] President Gordon, Mr. Koyé. . . . [*He bows ceremoniously.*] His Sacred Majesty, the Emperor, asks your presence.

[*Pause, all amazed.* KOYÉ *speaks in sudden triumph.*]

KOYÉ. One second out of all the centuries has called, and we have answered. Worlds have waited for this hour, and we have not failed. The myriad dead in every land, asleep in bloody and silent graves, they have not died in vain!

[*The two men clasp hands and hearts, as by a common impulse. The end has come.* GORDON *seems rapt, to be looking and thinking very far away. A smile of wistful wonder flits across his face, as he speaks words strangely and beautifully familiar.*]

GORDON. [*Slowly, very quietly, as though reading from some hidden scroll of memory.*] "Not by might, nor by power, but by my spirit, saith the Lord."

CURTAIN